The Discovery of New Mexico

Ad. I. Bandelier.

Adolph F. Bandelier's

The Discovery of New Mexico

by the Franciscan Monk,
Friar Marcos de Niza
in 1539

Translated from the French and edited,
with Introduction and Notes
by
Madeleine Turrell Rodack

University of Arizona Press
Tucson, Arizona

About the Editor . . .

MADELEINE TURRELL RODACK's keen interest in the history of the Hispanic Southwest, together with her bilingual ability, has uniquely prepared her to translate and edit the work of Adolph Bandelier. She holds degrees from Université de Paris and from the University of Washington. She obtained her Ph.D. in French and Spanish at the University of Arizona, where she made an extensive study of Antonin Artaud's visit to Mexico. This French actor-author's travels into remote Mexican lands led her to examine the Tarahumara Indians; their history and culture have since become one of her specialties. Always interested in tracing historic routes of famous explorers, she came upon the story of Fray Marcos de Niza while working on a translation of Bandelier's major work, the *Histoire de la Colonisation et des Missions de Sonora, Chihuahua, Nouveau Mexique et Arizona jusqu'a l'annee 1700*. A contributor to various southwestern historical journals, Dr. Rodack in 1975 became Assistant Ethnohistorian at the Arizona State Museum, University of Arizona.

THE UNIVERSITY OF ARIZONA PRESS

This book was set in 11/13 point Janson and 9/10 point Janson on a Videocomp 830.

Library of Congress Cataloging in Publication Data

Bandelier, Adolph Francis Alphonse, 1840-1914.
    Adolph F. Bandelier's The discovery of New Mexico by the Franciscan monk Friar Marcos de Niza in 1539.

    Translation of La découverte du Nouveau-Mexique, par le Moine franciscain frère Marcos, de Nice en 1539.
    Bibliography: p.
    Includes index.
    1. New Mexico—Discovery and exploration. 2. New Mexico—History—To 1848. 3. Southwest, New—Discovery and exploration.
4. Southwest, New—History—To 1848. 5. Indians of North America—New Mexico. 6. Indians of North America—Southwest, New.
7. Marco da Nizza, Father, ca. 1510-ca. 1570. I. Rodack, Madeleine Turrell.
II. Title. III. Title: Discovery of New Mexico
by the Franciscan monk Friar Marcos de Niza in 1539.
F799.B25513   978.9'01   80-25083
ISBN 0-8165-0717-1

Contents

Adolph F. Bandelier   Frontispiece

Maps

Foreword

Adolph F. Bandelier is one of those individuals whose accomplishments appear brighter and more important with the passage of time. In the period of his greatest productivity—from around 1880 through the first decade of the twentieth century—Bandelier, indeed, was recognized as a major figure in international scholarship. His great synthesis of Southwestern archaeology and ethnology, the *Final Report* (1890–92) was for many years *the* definitive work on the aboriginal Southwest. Bandelier also did extensive research in Mexico, and especially in western South America and produced, late in life, an important publication on the archaeology of the Lake Titicaca area (1910).

In spite of all this, following his death in Seville in 1914, Adolph Bandelier's work underwent a quarter century of neglect and eclipse. There was a plan in the 1930s to publish the voluminous daily journals that Bandelier kept for over twenty years, but this project, at the time, came to nothing.

During the year 1940 some note was made of the centennial of Bandelier's birth and that same year saw the publication by Leslie A. White of the Bandelier–Morgan correspondence. The major revival of interest in Bandelier's contribution to scholarly studies, however, dates from around 1960. In that year White and Ignacio Bernal brought out the Bandelier–García Icazbalceta correspondence and about that same time two colleagues

Charles H. Lange and Elizabeth M. Lange and I began preparing the Southwestern portions of the daily journals for publication. In 1964 Father Ernest J. Burrus discovered Bandelier's long lost *Histoire* manuscript, and this material is now being translated and annotated by Dr. Rodack.

An important reason for the renewed interest in Bandelier and his works is that new generations of scholars have a fuller appreciation of Bandelier as an early exponent of the interdisciplinary approach. Bandelier was not only an archaeologist, ethnologist, and historian but he was also interested in botany, geology, geography, and zoology, and incorporated all these fields into his anthropological and historical studies. Bandelier also saw clearly the interrelation of the parts of culture, their relationship to the history of the region, and to the natural environment. Especially in anthropology, Bandelier utilized a kind of structural–functional analysis, a sophisticated form of which has become fashionable in more recent times.

Bandelier not only made important contributions to anthropological and historical methodology; he was also the leading nineteenth century pioneer of ethnohistorical and archival studies of the early post–Columbian Southwest. Bandelier's combination of methodological sophistication and control of the archival data makes the Marcos de Niza paper important, not only as a landmark in Southwestern ethnohistory but as a work of scholarship in its own right. This French version of Marcos (far more detailed and much longer than the commonly cited English version) gives insights on Cabeza de Vaca, Marcos, and on early Southwestern exploration that are valid today. Since Bandelier lacked certain documents either physically not available to him or actually discovered later, the Marcos paper does contain minor errors. For example the word *Zuñi* (and close variants of it) which Bandelier thought was introduced by Oñate in 1598, was actually introduced in the early 1580s. In addition, Bandelier's statements on Southwestern Indian groups were made at a time when none of the groups had been well studied. Certain comments about relationships of tribes or languages need to be taken with some reservation.

These are caveats only, and do not distract from the importance of the work as a whole. Such important tasks as accurate tracing of the Marcos route have not been satisfactorily completed, and even the question as to whether Marcos ever actually reached Cíbola-Zuñi is still unanswered. Bandelier's speculations on these and other matters are quite viable today.

We are all much indebted to Madeleine T. Rodack, not only for her very readable translation but for the skillfully written introductory and annotative sections. Publication of the Marcos journey makes easily available to scholars (and people in general who are interested in the early Spanish Southwest) an important ethnohistoric document; one that continues to be a valuable source for study of this period.

CARROLL L. RILEY
Southern Illinois University

A Word from the Editor

The subject of Fray Marcos and the Seven Cities of Cíbola was a favorite of Adolph Bandelier. He discussed it in many of his writings, but rarely did he deal with it more completely or more clearly than in "La Découverte du Nouveau-Mexique par le moine Franciscain Frère Marcos de Nice en 1539," presented here for the first time in English.

On August 15, 1885, Bandelier, then settled in Santa Fe, wrote in his journal: "Got a letter from Dr. Eggert enclosing one from the Secretary of the Geographical Society of Paris about some publications which remunerate, at Paris." William Eggert was a Santa Fe doctor and close friend who was well aware of Bandelier's constant need for ways of making a living. Bandelier does not say whether any specific reference was made to the *Revue d'Ethnographie,* but in any case, the suggestion that a market existed for articles in French took root immediately. His French, however, was not the best. He apparently spoke the language well, but was not accustomed to writing it and always found this a chore. There are occasional obscurities and ambiguities in his turns of phrase. But in spite of his shortcomings, Bandelier went to work with a will and only two days after receiving Eggert's letter, his journal entry reads: "Began to write in French on the Discovery of New Mexico by Fray Marcos de Niza." He had just completed a series in German for the *New Yorker Staatszeitung* entitled "Cíbola" (Bandelier 1885); so the subject was fresh in his mind. This series appeared later in English as part of *The Gilded Man* (Bandelier 1893).

After this, there are occasional references to the work and to a James Jackson in Paris, who was presumably the Secretary referred to by Eggert. He notes that he finished the text of "Fray Marcos" on September 5, and an entry the following day reports sending the whole manuscript off to Paris on September 7.

The *Revue d'Ethnographie* printed the article in three installments in the issues of January–February, March–April and May–June, 1886. The chapter divisions here correspond to these three installments, but the titles to the chapters have been added by the editor-translator. The article was later translated into Spanish by a friend of Bandelier, Dr. Zabala, who was often mentioned in his journal, and published in *El Boletín Popular,* a Santa Fe newspaper, from January 17 to March 7, 1889.

Perhaps the work done on this article inspired Bandelier to write a shorter English paper on Fray Marcos published in the *Magazine of Western History* of September, 1886, and reprinted in the *New Mexico Historical Review* in 1929 (Vol. II, No. 8). The French article has often been referred to as merely a version of the English one, but they are in fact quite different. The English text is comparatively brief—Bandelier mentions it as being only thirteen pages long—and does not discuss at any length the part that Cabeza de Vaca's adventures might have played in inspiring the Fray Marcos expedition. He wrote it in two days, whereas the French article took him three weeks.

The text as printed in the *Revue d'Ethnographie* is not entirely accurate. Typographical errors are numerous. Unfortunately, Bandelier's original manuscript no longer exists, and the printed article is all that remains to us. The notes, as in all of Bandelier's writings, are voluminous, with extensive quotations from the original Spanish. Bandelier's meticulous and scholarly mind was such that he insisted that the original text be placed at the reader's disposal so that those who knew Spanish well enough could draw their conclusions directly from his sources. At the risk of opposing Bandelier's intention, these passages are presented here in English translation so that all readers may benefit.

Since most of the editions used by Bandelier are not definitely identified or are unavailable, the page numbers he gives as references often will not apply. However, some may be located and all have been included in case any reader should wish to consult the Spanish text, and be fortunate enough to discover the rare editions referred to. In several instances the Spanish original was apparently unavailable to Bandelier and he was obliged to work with a French translation, hence the French titles of some of the Spanish works.

In his notes, Bandelier generally uses the Spanish abbreviations "lib" and "cap" for "book" and "chapter." These have not been translated, but have been retained as they appear in the text. The abbreviations that Bandelier used have been retained as well, and merely converted to their English equivalents. Bandelier's spellings of place names in the text and notes have also been preserved. Elsewhere, more modern spellings have been adopted wherever a difference exists.

The bibliography lists primarily works that have a direct historical bearing on the stories of Cabeza de Vaca and Fray Marcos and on Bandelier himself, and includes many not specifically referred to either in the main text or in the introductory material. Thus, it is intended as a working bibliography for those who may care to pursue further the subject of Fray Marcos' journey. However, it is also a selected one and does not pretend to be complete. For the most part, works dealing with specialized archaeological and ethnological studies have not been included. Nor does the bibliography contain all the references mentioned by Bandelier in his notes, though a number of these will nevertheless be found listed, usually in a more modern edition, as works of general information.

Acknowledgments

I am grateful for the assistance of Charles W. Polzer and Bernard L. Fontana, both of whom read the introductory material and made useful suggestions, and to Daniel S. Matson, who assisted me with the interpretation of German sources and with some fine points of Spanish translation. In addition Carroll L. Riley contributed several helpful bits of criticism. I appreciate the hospitality and the information offered me by T. J. Ferguson and Barbara Mills, resident archaeologists at Zuñi. I am greatly indebted to my husband, Juel Rodack, who not only acted as a critic, but also did some of the groundwork for the maps accompanying this work. These maps have been rendered in final form by Don Bufkin. Finally, I wish to thank the University of Arizona Press for undertaking the publication of this book.

MADELEINE TURRELL RODACK

Part One

Bandelier and the Search for Cibola

Adolph Francis Alphonse Bandelier

What relationship could the small town of Highland, Illinois, where Bandelier grew up, possibly have to the Indian lands of New Mexico and their exploration by Fray Marcos de Niza? Yet in the work of Adolph Bandelier these two worlds did meet. The exact point at which he became interested in Mexican history and ethnology is uncertain. His younger years were spent as an employee in his father's bank and he may well have been approaching thirty before he became deeply involved with the Spanish historical chronicles. In any case, from Bandelier himself we learn that "the aboriginal history of Spanish America had always been my desire." (White 1940, p. 74, note 22: Letter to C. E. Norton, Sept. 18, 1887.)

Adolph Francis Alphonse Bandelier was born on August 6, 1840, in Switzerland. His family home was in Canton Berne and it has been said that, as a small child, he lived in a castle. In any case, his father, Adolphe Eugene Bandelier, came from a prominent family. A member of the Superior Court in his home country, the elder Bandelier was politically involved. Though a scholarly man of broad interests, he apparently found himself in an uncomfortable political position in 1847, after the Sonderbund war. Deciding to seek a new home beyond the Swiss borders, he left his family behind, and with a friend, John Balsinger, traveled to Brazil to explore possibilities there. However, they did not find it to their liking and ended up in Highland, Illinois, among the rolling green hills only a few miles east of St. Louis. Many Swiss had settled there; in fact, it was originally known as "New Switzerland." The men from Berne immediately felt at home.

The elder Bandelier sent for his family and they arrived in 1848, when young Adolph was eight, bringing with them even the family maid. His mother, Marie Senn, had been married before to a Swiss army officer and with him had visited Russia on several occasions. Widowed when quite young, she later married Adolphe Eugene Bandelier. They had only one child. Marie never really adapted to the new way of life and died seven years after her arrival in the United States. She is the sole member of the family to be buried in Highland, in the Sonnenberg Cemetery.

The boy was educated mainly at home. His principal tutor, besides his father, was a young native of Lyon, Timothy Gruaz, who had gone to school in Lausanne. Gruaz later worked for the bank in which the elder Bandelier was a partner with two local businessmen, Frederick Ryhiner and Moritz Huegy, Sr. It was natural that his tutor should be French because Bandelier had spoken this language since earliest childhood, and refers to it as his "native tongue." (See letter to C. E. Norton, referred to above.) However, he was also fluent in German and in later years seemed to prefer it for many of his writings. Though German was spoken in the family much of the time, he and his father often conversed in French, and Bandelier always insisted on the French pronunciation of his name (Bahn-duh-lee-ā).

The young man grew up on the Highland farm purchased by his father. The Bandeliers did not work the farm themselves, but employed others to do so. With its house standing on a high hill overlooking the town, the property had the appearance of an estate. Adolph helped out in the bank and participated in the social life of the community; both he and his father were active in many civic enterprises. In 1862 he married Josephine Huegy, the daughter of one of his father's partners. He led the life of an average well-to-do citizen of a typical midwestern town.

But much more was taking place beneath the surface. Very early Bandelier had become interested in various sciences such as mineralogy, geology, and meteorology. However, the pressures of the business world, which he thoroughly disliked, prevented him from carrying on regular scientific observations in these fields, so he turned to the Mexican documents as a relief from the hated daily chores. To pursue the study of Spanish America he needed to know Spanish and managed to learn it through his own efforts. In a letter of November 9, 1875 (White and Bernal 1960, p. 112), he mentions that two years ago he knew no Spanish at all. But, during a short stay in the hospital, he procured a Spanish historical work that interested him and started to read it without even the help of a dictionary. He continued this method with other works and learned the language simply through reading. Bandelier's knowledge of French certainly contributed to this accomplishment.

Around 1873, Bandelier met Lewis H. Morgan and a lengthy correspondence followed. Morgan was a pioneer in the study of ethnology and anthropology. He had specialized in the Iroquois and presented the theory that the "civilized" Indians of Mexico, such as the Aztecs and Mayas, had in reality been little more advanced in their organization than the more "primitive" Indians. Morgan believed that civilizations progressed from a type of society based only on personal relations, which he called a "societas," to more advanced types of social organization based on land and property, thus constituting a state. This Morgan called a "civitas." No Indians had ever reached that point, according to Morgan. The "societas" was the limit of even the most advanced native peoples.

The older scholar became interested in Bandelier and gradually converted him to his own way of thinking. And indeed, in 1877, when the younger man began to publish monographs on the ancient Mexicans, he showed strong support for Morgan's point of view. It was from Morgan that Bandelier got the idea that historical documents should not be accepted at their face value, but that field work, excavation, and study of Indian life should be carried on to substantiate or correct the information in the chronicles. Thus Bandelier's research developed a whole new dimension, leading to a situation in which his business activities inhibited the pursuit of this new work even more than they had his scientific observations.

In spite of being anchored to Highland and the bank, in 1877 he began to write. Relying purely on periodic library research in St. Louis, and on books borrowed wherever possible, Bandelier managed to publish several monographs on the ancient Mexicans, as well as various book reviews. His work made such an impression that, after his health broke down due to conflict between his duties at the bank and his real interests, he was offered an opportunity to go to Santa Fe under auspices of the Archaeological Institute of America. In August 1880, Adolph Bandelier began what he felt was his true life's work. He was 40 years old.

Writing from Highland in 1877 to Frederick W. Putnam, Curator of the Peabody Museum at Harvard, Bandelier referred to himself as "one who had no opportunity to travel." After 1880 he could never again complain of this. He often journeyed from Santa Fe to the various Indian villages and Pueblo ruins in New Mexico, and spent some time living with the natives in the towns of Santo Domingo and Cochití. He returned to Highland at the end of the year, but was off again in 1881 for Mexico, this time as representative of the Archaeological Institute of America on the Lorillard Expedition financed by the tobacco millionaire in conjunction with the French government. However, when he arrived in Mexico he found the expedition ready to abandon its plans and return to France. Nevertheless, his agreement with its supporters afforded him the means to remain and visit many historic sites on which he reported to the Archaeological Institute (Bandelier 1884).

Bandelier was in Santa Fe again the following year and again toured the surrounding Indian country. In 1883, he made trips to Arizona and El Paso as well. He visited northern Mexico in 1884, crossing from Sonora to Chihuahua on horseback, in spite of an Apache threat. All this was interspersed with several trips to Highland.

Meanwhile, the bank was not doing well due to some unwise investments, and Bandelier made a journey to Europe at the end of 1884 to try to raise loans among his father's connections and to placate Swiss creditors. He was unsuccessful on both counts, and in 1885, F. Ryhiner and Co. was on the brink of failure. The bank closed on April 30 and Bandelier, who was in Highland at the time, was one of those held responsible. His father left town abruptly for South America, leaving his son to face the charges along with the sons of the original partners, Moritz Huegy, Jr. and Frederick Ryhiner, Jr. The latter son, however, departed within a few days for Iowa where he had relatives. He did return later, but only after the worst was over.

Huegy, despondent in the face of accusations against him, committed suicide within the month, and Bandelier was arrested as the only remaining responsible person. He was held in jail for one night in Edwardsville, the county seat, before being released on bond. Huegy and Ryhiner had inherited their fathers' partnerships in the bank, but Bandelier was not a partner. He felt that he was in no way responsible; nevertheless, the full burden of the "crime" fell on him. He had no alternative but to sign over all his property to the creditors, including the family home and farm where he had lived as a boy. Yet to this day, many people in Highland insist that he "stole" money from the bank to finance his field trips, a claim that has little to substantiate it.

From that time on, Bandelier and his wife, Joe (as she was always called), decided to settle in Santa Fe, but his travels continued. He journeyed to Mexico City to work in the archives there, made his usual rounds among the New Mexican Indian ruins and pueblos, visited El Paso and Denver, returned to Mexico City in 1890 and went to the east coast in 1892.

During these years he continued his research, copying documents wherever he could find them. He wrote constantly, as this was his major means of livelihood. In the midst of his struggles his father reappeared from Venezuela where he had taken refuge. The older man moved in with the Bandeliers in Santa Fe, and, though he did help with his son's work mainly by doing copying jobs for him, he was not easy to live with and added to the household's problems. Bandelier had new responsibilities, and life was much harder than he was accustomed to in his youth.

The now established scholar desperately wanted to spend more time in Mexico and to work in the archives in Spain, but he had no means of financing such projects. His labors in New Mexico had been backed mainly by the Archaeological Institute of America, but in 1885 this organization was short of funds and no longer willing to support his research. He sold an occasional article whenever possible and was delighted when, in 1886, Archbishop Salpointe offered him $1,500 to write a history of the Spanish Borderlands. It was to be a gift from the Archdiocese of Santa Fe to Pope Leo XIII for the pontiff's Golden Jubilee. This history is the extensive work in French now in the Vatican Library, the *Histoire de la Colonisation et des Missions de Sonora, Chihuahua, Nouveau-Mexique et Arizona jusqu'à l'année 1700,* completed at the end of 1887. This manuscript has never been published, but has recently been translated into English at the University of Arizona by the editor of the present volume. Publication plans are in progress at the time of this writing. (See Bandelier 1887.)

During these difficult years Bandelier was offered a position as historian for the Hemenway expedition, organized to study southwestern archaeology, and headed by his friend Frank Hamilton Cushing. This, at least, allowed him to continue his research in New Mexico and to make a trip to New York City. But after six years, this source of revenue gave out. Bandelier had hoped to gain some income from his novel, *The Delight Makers* (first written in German), a fascinating and educational tale of the prehistoric inhabitants of the Rito de los Frijoles, which is now a part of Bandelier National Monument. However, even after translation and publication in English, it was no great success. In 1892, Bandelier found himself in desperate straits. Then came the opportunity to head the Villard expedition to Peru and Bolivia. In spite of his greater interest in Mexico and desire to go to Spain, Bandelier jumped at the chance for a steady income. In May of 1892 he and his wife left for California to board a ship for South America.

As usual Bandelier managed to cover a great deal of ground both in Peru and later in Bolivia. However, his travels were at first delayed by his wife's illness and death in December of the same year. Bandelier then devoted himself completely to his work. He was more interested in exploring archives and visiting remote ruins than in collecting antiquities for his employer. This pattern did not change when, in 1894, the Museum of Natural History took over his support. A year after Joe's death, he married Fanny Ritter, also of Swiss heritage, whom he had met in La Paz, Bolivia. She was a tremendous help to him in the years that followed, since she was also gifted in languages and had scholarly talents almost equal to his own.

Bandelier spent 10 years in South America. He and Fanny returned to New York in 1903, where he continued to arrange his notes for the Museum and gave numerous lectures. In 1906, more publications followed under the auspices of the Hispanic Society of America. He worked now with a handicap; his eyesight was failing and he had to rely on Fanny to assist him. He was nevertheless appointed a research assistant for the Carnegie Institution in 1911.

When his vision improved after a cataract operation, he and his wife returned to Mexico to collect archival material. In 1913 they returned to New York but left soon afterwards for Spain to do similar work. At last Bandelier was realizing his dream, but the realization was short-lived. Within two months of starting to work in the Archives of Seville, he became seriously ill. He died and was buried there in March of 1914. Only recently have his remains been returned to Santa Fe. Fanny stayed in Spain until 1915 to carry on with the work that he had begun.

What sort of a man was Bandelier? Existing pictures represent him as quite a serious person. He was always formally dressed, with jacket, tie, and stiff collar. Even field photographs, showing him among ruins or in front of ancient churches, rarely represent him casually attired. His traveling costume, according to Will C. Barnes, was quite picturesque. In *Apaches and Longhorns*, Barnes described Bandelier as he rode into Fort Apache in April of 1883, after having been reported killed by Apache Indians.

> He was a singular figure. On his head was a genuine Scottish bonnet, the Glengarry, with two ribbons hanging down behind. He wore a Norfolk Jacket, knickerbockers of rough tweed, and heavy English walking shoes—a costume that would have attracted attention almost anywhere west of the Mississippi River, and certainly so on the Indian frontier in Arizona Territory.
>
> He was mounted on a diminutive yellow mule. A vast Spanish saddle almost covered the beast, which was not much bigger than a burro. The rider's long legs just missed the ground. On the pommel of the saddle was a pair of large Spanish *cantinas;* and at the cantle a roll of blankets inside of which were all his earthly possessions. (Barnes 1941, pp. 105–106.)

When Barnes wrote this in later years his imagination may have influenced him, and the description may not be completely accurate. Bandelier's mount, for example, was actually a small horse rather than a mule. However, Bandelier's traveling costume may have been unusual enough to have left a colorful impression on Barnes. Far from wishing to ridicule Bandelier, the then youthful army telegrapher admired him greatly. Later when a name was sought for the National Monument in New Mexico, it was Barnes' suggestion that it be named for Bandelier.

Though Bandelier appeared serious in pictures, he nevertheless possessed a touch of humor which appears occasionally in his writings, especially in his journal. He enjoyed company, and was particularly fond of joining his friends at "the brewery" and attending literary and social gatherings, though he seemed to care less for community picnics and civic celebrations which he was often called upon to attend in Highland.

As a worker he was indefatigable. During his years at the bank he studied and wrote whenever he could find the time. He pushed himself until his health gave way. This was ultimately a good thing, for it gave him an excuse to leave the bank and devote himself to his own interests. Free to work in his chosen field, he enjoyed his labors except when he was forced to write for money. He was spoiled and accustomed to the good life as a child, and when things went badly, he became temporarily bitter toward people who meant him no harm. However, when the crisis was over, he would shower the same people with compliments. He had no trouble acquiring devoted friends.

Bandelier had never appeared very devout, though with his first wife he had attended Protestant services in Highland. However, in 1881, in Mexico, he became a Catholic. It has been said that he took this step to gain easier access to Church records, useful in his work. However, there is no real reason to assume this. He unquestionably did attend Mass often, even when his wife, Joe, was still going to the Protestant church in Santa Fe. He paid more than lip service to the Catholic Church and made close friends among the New Mexico clergy; one of these friends was Archbishop Salpointe.

In spite of his protected youth, he never feared hardships in the field. He traveled many miles in remote places where the comforts of civilization were unknown, and was so thoroughly absorbed in his work that he never spared himself, keeping at it unrelentingly until the last days of his life.

The list of Bandelier's writings is quite voluminous. The Peabody Museum published his first articles on various aspects of the life of the ancient Mexicans (1877–1880). Most of his major works were written for the Archaeological Institute of America. His first archaeological manuscript, *A Visit to the Aboriginal Ruins in the Valley of the Río Pecos* (1881), and an early anthropological monograph, *Historical Introduction to Studies among the Sedentary Indians of New Mexico* (1881) appeared under their auspices as did his *Report of an Archaeological Tour in Mexico* (1884). *Contributions to the History of the Southwestern Portion of the United States* (1890*a*) was also written for that organization. His most lengthy publication for the Archaeological Institute of America was the *Final Report of Investigations among the Indians of the Southwestern United States,* which he worked on periodically for many years and which was finally published in 1890–92. He also published a large number of book reviews and articles in English and German, and an occasional one in French, on a wide variety of subjects. The papal gift from the Archdiocese of Santa Fe, the still unpublished *Histoire* mentioned above, rivaled the *Final Report* in length. In 1890, his only novel, *The Delight Makers,* appeared. In 1893, a collection of historical studies, *The Gilded Man,* was published. This list is only a partial one. Considering that all his writing was done during the last half of his life, his output is truly impressive.

One little-known aspect of his work is his numerous drawings and illustrations. Bandelier's journal includes many sketches, primarily of Indian ruins, but these are simple and served him merely as reminders. Some diagrams of ruins are also included in his book on Pecos and in the *Final Report.* But his true talent as an artist appears in the *Histoire.* As part of the gift to the pope, Bandelier included many drawings that he had made over the years, to which he added numerous new sketches of ground plans of various ancient Indian pueblos, Indian costumes and headdresses, examples of house construction, dance patterns, details of petroglyphs, artifacts of all kinds, and pottery with finely reproduced designs. These are all in exquisite watercolor.

A few have already been presented in Ernest J. Burrus' *Supplement* to his introductory volume for the planned French edition of the *Histoire* (*A Catalogue of the Bandelier Collection in the Vatican Library*), which has not been completed. Hopefully the entire collection will finally appear when the English version of this work is published (Bandelier 1887).

Adolph Bandelier was professionally a self-trained man. Today he might have been considered an amateur having had no formal schooling in his field. In his day, however, there was little instruction available in such subjects as archaeology, anthropology, and ethnology. The early Spanish historical documents were only beginning to be studied and published. The best system was to read everything possible and to sit at the feet of the master. Becoming a "disciple" of Morgan was what really set Bandelier on his way.

When he first went to New Mexico he knew nothing about practical archaeology, and his methods of measuring ruins and sending back samples of everything in sight may seem primitive. Bandelier learned as he went. His capacity for assembling information was unlimited and his constant archival work established a strong background for field work. Conversely, the field work provided physical evidence to complete the information learned from his beloved chronicles and archival documents.

Adolph Bandelier was a pioneer in the then vast general domain that covered history, archaeology, anthropology, and ethnology. In the days before specialization, he was a "universal man" in the study of the peoples, places, and history of the ancient Southwest.

Fray Marcos de Niza and the Search for Cíbola

In the Province of New Spain, during the reign of Carlos V, an event took place that was to have greater repercussions than anyone then living could ever have imagined. In fact, the judgment of its contemporaries pronounced it a failure. The year was 1539; the event was the discovery of Cíbola by the Franciscan monk Fray Marcos de Niza.

Columbus, in seeking a passage to the Orient, had dreams of gold and great treasure. Quicker access to the riches of Cathay was the major purpose of Spain's earliest expedition across the unknown ocean. The discovery of only a few Indians did not destroy the explorer's belief that these riches were at hand and that other hidden treasures lay somewhere beyond. Cortés' conquest of the Aztec people and their ruler Montezuma seemed to justify this belief, for gold was indeed found in their city of Tenochtitlan. Pizarro had equal or greater good fortune in Peru. The treasure did exist. But, the acquisition of so much gold by the conquerors did not enrich them personally as much as they had hoped, and only served to spur them on. A large amount of the wealth went into the royal treasury which constantly needed replenishing. So, all those involved, unsatisfied and believing that they were on the trail of greater things, became even more desperate to push forward and discover the great golden cities of Cíbola of which legend had for many years extolled the glory.

Since ancient times it seems these legends had been rife. The seven golden cities lay always just beyond the reach of the explorers and adventurers who sought them. They vaulted over the ocean from a mysterious Atlantic mini-continent, never discovered and eventually bypassed, to the islands of the Caribbean, and, as each of these was in turn revealed, to the mainland itself. The dream stayed one step ahead of Spanish penetration and, as new lands opened up, moved farther and farther into regions still unknown, spurring on the fortune hunters, like the proverbial carrot dangling before the donkey.

By the year 1538 the famous cities were thought to be in the North, beyond the borders of New Spain. As Spanish expansion pushed northward, stories began to spread about cities of gold and "people who wore cotton." At this point Cabeza de Vaca's journey across Texas added fuel to the fire, for he implied that Indians told him of such cities. Shipwrecked in Florida, he and his three companions spent eight long years reaching their compatriots in Mexico. They had talked with many Indians, heard many stories and their contemporaries felt they were in a position to know. The Franciscan friar, Marcos de Niza, appeared on the scene, chosen to verify the legend and bear witness to the existence of the gold.

Fray Marcos was presumably born in Nice, as his name implies; no other name for him has ever been mentioned. His native city was in what was then the Duchy of Savoy, associated historically with Italy, but many French lived there—the region is now part of France—and Fray Marcos was one of these. In 1539, Fray Jerónimo Ximénez de San Esteban wrote in a letter to Father Tomás de Villanueva in Burgos: "It was a year ago this last September that a friar of San Francisco, French by nationality, left this City of Mexico, in search of a country which the governor of these parts has heard about and has not been able to explore." (García-Icazbalceta 1882–92, vol. I, p. 194.) The priest might have been more correctly referred to as "Frère Marc de Nice," but, since he served the Spaniards in the New World, he became known as Fray Marcos de Niza.

The date of his entrance into the Franciscan order is uncertain, though 1531 has been mentioned as a possibility. This date, however, given by Fray Agustín de Vetancurt in his *Menologio Franciscano* (Vetancurt 1961), more likely merely refers to Fray Marcos' departure for the New World. How old he was at the time and where he went first are unknown. Various stories claim that it was either to Hispaniola or to Nicaragua. The latter is perhaps more logical, as Fray Marcos eventually traveled to Peru and could have gone there as a follower of Sebastián Belalcázar. Pizarro called this conqueror of Nicaragua to Peru to govern San Miguel and later appointed him governor of Quito which he had personally subjected.

Bartolomé de Las Casas offers a different version of the story in his *Brevíssima Relacíon* (Las Casas 1974). Las Casas quotes a document transmitted to him, he says, by Bishop Zumárraga, in which Fray Marcos testifies to many atrocities committed by the Spaniards in Peru. The Franciscan states that he was among the first to go there, giving us the impression that he may have gone with Francisco Pizarro. However, this seems unlikely since the Pizarro expedition left Panama in January of 1531 and Fray Marcos could hardly have been in the New World that early.

Fray Marcos says that he can testify that the Inca Atahualpa was treacherously executed by the Spaniards, but does not claim that he actually saw it (Las Casas 1974). So, whether he was there with Pizarro at that time or not is still questionable.

Another hypothesis is that the friar's original assignment, or at least an early one, was Guatemala. According to Henry Wagner in *The Spanish Southwest* (Part I, p. 47) a document drawn up in that country in 1536, in which Fray Marcos gives testimony, states that he went south with Pedro de Alvarado, governor of Guatemala. This expedition, to conquer Quito in January 1533, was foiled because Belalcázar had preceded him. In this document in the Archives of the Indies, Fray Marcos states that he served under Alvarado as a messenger to Diego de Almagro, Pizarro's associate, who had confronted Alvarado's expedition and negotiated a peaceful settlement with him. Fray Marcos presumably remained with Alvarado, accompanying him on a visit to Pizarro and back to Guatemala. In any case, the document would show that Fray Marcos was in that country and acting as a witness for Alvarado in 1536.

Another possibility is that Fray Marcos made two trips to Peru. In 1531 Nicaragua was a staging area for friars assigned to Peru, so it is quite possible that he did go there first. Antonine Tibesar, in his *Franciscan Beginnings in Colonial Peru* (Tibesar 1953), points out several references to a commissary and five friars setting out from Nicaragua for Peru at that time, which could coincide with Belalcázar's journey to take over the government of San Miguel. This agrees with Fray Marcos' statement that he was "comisario" of the Franciscans in Peru and could place him there with Belalcázar.

Tibesar refers to a letter of February 25, 1532 from Panama telling of the recent return of "the Franciscans who went from Nicaragua to Peru," bringing accounts of atrocities being committed there. Marcos could have been one of this group. It would then have been quite possible for the friar to return to Peru with Alvarado's expedition in 1534. This would explain his association with the governor of Guatemala and his testimony on the latter's behalf.

All the conflicting statements have not been satisfactorily reconciled. All we really know is that the friar did spend some time in Peru and did witness some of the unfortunate events there.

Friar Marcos referred to himself as a "comisario" in Peru, charged with providing for a small group of religious men which was normally formed in the early days of a colony. However, the missions to Peru became numerous enough in a few years to constitute a "custodia." Archbishop Zumárraga mentions in a letter written in 1537 that Fray Marcos was then in Mexico and that he had been elected "custodio" by the friars in Peru. The priest was later named "provincial" of the Mexican province, a "provincia" being the next highest level of ecclesiastical organization.

In 1537 Marcos returned to Guatemala, shocked at the atrocities committed by the Spaniards in Peru and wrote to Zumárraga from there. He went to Mexico City at the Archbishop's request. There is also reference in the Zumárraga letter to a "relación" by Fray Marcos concerning events in Peru which he felt displayed extreme cruelty by those who professed to be Christians. Zumárraga implied that a report should be sent to the king and further cruelties prevented. The friar, however, was so busy with sermons and confessions, according to Zumárraga, that nothing had yet been done. Nevertheless, in 1538, when an experienced explorer was sought in Mexico, Fray Marcos de Niza was at hand.

But the viceroy, Don Antonio de Mendoza, did not immediately turn to Fray Marcos. His first thought was to attempt to mount an expedition to the North headed by at least one of Cabeza de Vaca's party, who were experienced in travel among the savage tribes. Cabeza de Vaca himself looked forward to returning to Spain, and his companion Alonso del Castillo Maldonado had other projects in mind. Only Andrés Dorantes and his slave Estevan remained, and Mendoza decided to send Dorantes as head of an expedition. Apparently the viceroy did gather the equipment together, but the journey was never made. Mendoza himself states in a letter to the king (Mendoza 1864–84; Hammond and Rey 1940, pp. 51–52) that he did not know why the plan collapsed.

However, the viceroy did not abandon his determination to verify the legends of the North. Some controversy exists as to his next step. The story goes that two other Franciscan priests set out a year earlier to explore the northern coast. This tale probably started with the account given in the *Historia de los Indios de la Nueva-España* by Fray Toribio Paredes de Benavente, better known as Motolinía, that two friars were sent north in 1538, accompanied by a captain. The captain chose a route to the right which proved so rugged that he had to turn back. The friars turned to the left and covered 300 leagues, coming to a great river which they could not cross. They encountered people such as Fray Marcos describes, and were treated by them in much the same manner as he was. The story is very similar to that of Fray Marcos. One of the friars even falls ill as did Fray Marcos' companion. The captain could have been Coronado who, while the friar was away, made a short journey into the mountains. Motolinía wrote this report at the time when de Niza had just returned from his journey. It seems that he is actually telling part of Fray Marcos' story, though, strangely, he mentions no names and it is peculiar that he did not refer to the discovery of Cíbola, unless, of course, he did not believe it had occurred. For these reasons many scholars think that Motolinía was speaking of a preceding expedition.

The story has been repeated many times over the years, but may have merely been copied from Motolinía. Fray Gerónimo de Mendieta recounts it in almost the same words in his *Historia Ecclesiastica Indiana*, over 50 years later. Mendieta adds, however, that Fray Marcos, hearing of this expedition, set out himself to verify it. It is interesting that Mendieta mentions actually meeting Fray Marcos later, and thus could have obtained first-hand information.

The story appeared again in the *Monarchía Indiana* of Fray Juan de Torquemada in 1615, and is told by Fray Zárate-Salmerón in 1626 and by Fray Agustín de Vetancurt near the end of the seventeenth century.

Only in the eighteenth century did these mysterious monks acquire names. Added information may have been based on other documents now lost. In 1720, Captain Juan Mateo Manje, companion of the celebrated Father Eusebio Francisco Kino, makes a certain Fray Juan de la Asunción the hero of the story. Next, Matías de la Mota-Padilla included the account in his *Historia de la Nueva Galicia* in 1742; the priest is called Fray Juan de Olmeda, and again Fray Marcos is said to have set out to verify the story, taking Olmeda with him.

Father Francisco Garcés writes in a diary of his travels in 1775-76 that a Juan de la Asunción had been sent by Fray Marcos, who at about that time had been named "provincial." In 1792, the historian Fray Juan Domingo Arricivita states that two friars, Juan de la Asunción and Pedro Nadal, traveled 600 leagues to the north. He skips Fray Marcos' trip mentioning him only as going with three other friars on a military expedition (probably Coronado's, which he did in fact accompany). Presumably, de la Asumpción and de la Asunción are one and the same.

So the question of whether or not there was an exploration by Franciscan friars previous to Fray Marcos' is controversial. The story could have originated in Motolinía's rather incomplete account, which may have been intended to refer to Fray Marcos, or it may be based on documents now lost that actually

gave names and facts concerning an earlier exploration. Bandelier feels that the story is well founded and that such a trip did
indeed take place.

In any case, if unknown friars made such a journey, the
consensus is that they did not get farther than the Gila River,
which might have been the great river that they were unable to
cross. Thus, any possible earlier expedition into southern
Arizona definitely did not penetrate as far as New Mexico.

Viceroy Antonio de Mendoza kept firmly to his purpose, but
he was too cautious a man to mount a full-fledged military
expedition, especially after the Dorantes fiasco, without better
proof that the cities he sought really existed. So he turned at last
to Fray Marcos de Niza who was in Mexico City under the
patronage of Archbishop Zumárraga. Though Marcos was presumably recommended by the "provincial," Antonio de Ciudad-
Rodrigo, it is even possible that the archbishop suggested him
for the task, for Zumárraga never ceased to take an interest in
Marcos de Niza to the end of his days. Thus, in the fall of 1538
the Franciscan was sent to Culiacán from Mexico City and given
instructions, equipment, and an escort for the journey.

Mendoza surely felt it was a stroke of genius to send the black
slave Estevan along, who had been through it all before with
Cabeza de Vaca's expedition and "knew the ropes" so to speak.
He was the best alternative to Dorantes, but, being a slave, could
not be put in charge of the expedition. Early in the trip Fray
Marcos sent him ahead to gather information, and this in fact
made him a leader. Though he did not neglect the friar who was
following and always saw to it that the way was prepared,
Estevan began to feel a freedom that he had never known. He
went off, in charge of his personal following of Indians, and
"forgot" to return or even wait, as Fray Marcos had ordered
him. This, unfortunately for him, later led to disaster and
death.

Bandelier tells the tale of Fray Marcos' journey and Estevan's
demise quite graphically. He bases it on the Franciscan's own
Relación and quotes him at length. There was little else he could
base it on except for brief references to the expedition by the
various historians mentioned above. The only other complete
account is given by Antonio de Herrera around 1600, in his
Historia general de los hechos de los Castellanos en las Islas y Tierra

Firma del Mar Océano. Herrera practically gives a word for word rendering of Marcos' *Relación,* recast into the third person.

As Bandelier points out, there was probably another more complete and scientific account written by Fray Marcos. The monk implies its existence when he speaks of the Indians' reports on the coastal islands "the names of which I am writing in another paper where I am recording the names of the islands and settlements" (Hammond and Rey 1940, p. 67; Pacheco y Cárdenas 1864–84, Vol. 3, Ser. I, p. 262). What vistas might be opened to historians if that document should come to light! The great controversy over the Fray Marcos expedition might then be solved.

Just after the middle of the nineteenth century the question of the location of Cíbola was raised, which might help to determine the friar's route. Lewis H. Morgan, the "father of anthropology" and good friend of Bandelier, attempted to prove that Cíbola was the group of villages that includes Pueblo Bonito, in the area now in the Chaco Canyon National Monument of northwestern New Mexico (see Morgan 1869). About the same time, James H. Simpson suggested Zuñi, but he believed Cíbola to be one of its villages of which he found the ruins on top of the great mesa known as Toyoalana, which Bandelier refers to as "Thunder Mountain" (see Simpson 1871). These villages were sometimes called "Old Zuñi" and their location in no way corresponds to Fray Marcos' description of Cíbola as being situated "en un llano a la falda de un cerro redondo" (on a plain on the slope of a round height). W. W. H. Davis (Davis 1869) agrees with Simpson as to the general area of Zuñi, but places Cíbola on the site of the present Zuñi pueblo, formerly called Hálona. This too has been referred to as "Old Zuñi" which further confuses the matter.

In discussing his German translation of Fray Marcos' *Relación,* Martin Gusinde also concurs with this theory (Gusinde 1942–43), stating, strangely, that the friar viewed Cíbola from the top of Thunder Mountain, though he does not explain how de Niza could have climbed such tortuous trails to reach that isolated vantage point, especially considering his haste and anxiety. In any case, Hálona seems an unlikely choice, for though it does lie on a plain, the rise on which it stands is hardly high enough to qualify as a "cerro."

Bandelier also took Cíbola down from the mountain, but kept it on the slopes of Toyoalana, for he believed it was the village of Qaquima. In 1895, Frederick W. Hodge presented his theory that Cíbola was the pueblo of Hawikuh. This view is now generally accepted in spite of its opposition to the Zuñi legends, which Hodge dismisses rather cavalierly, but which agree with Bandelier. The ruins of Hawikuh still stand, though increasingly less evident, near the hot springs at Ojo Caliente (which Bandelier refers to as "Aguas Calientes"), about fifteen miles southwest of Zuñi pueblo. The idea of Qaquima is, however, continually repeated by Bandelier in later treatments of the subject: in the English article on Fray Marcos (Bandelier 1886c), in *The Gilded Man,* in the still unpublished *Histoire de la Colonisation et des Missions* . . . (Bandelier 1887), and elsewhere.

Thus, the subject of the location of Cíbola has been discussed at length and with occasional rancor. It is fairly well agreed, however, that it was one of the Zuñi pueblos. Most historians and archaeologists accept Hodge's identification, but, in view of the nature of the terrain and the interpretation of the word "cerro" (which implies a greater height than the mere "hill" by which students of Fray Marcos usually translate it), Bandelier's theory is not an impossible one. It is a subject that could stand some reconsideration.

Assuming that Cíbola was one of the Zuñi villages, the route by which Fray Marcos arrived there was also an early subject of speculation. As long ago as the end of the seventeenth century, Father Eusebio Francisco Kino made one of the first judgments about it when, as Bandelier points out, he believed he had identified Vacapa, one of Fray Marcos' major stops, as Bacapa, northeast of the head of the Gulf of California, not far from the Arizona-Sonora border and now associated with Quitovac. (See Stocklein 1726, map, p. 52 and *Lettres édifiantes et curieuses* 1754, map, Vol. I, p. 52.) This led to a school of thought that took Fray Marcos northwest along the coast to Altar, passing near Tucson and perhaps Phoenix. One of the strongest advocates of this theory is George J. Undreiner, who discusses such a route in "Fray Marcos de Niza and his Journey to Cíbola" (Undreiner 1947).

Undreiner even claims that, if Marcos followed the westerly route, the controversial side trip to observe the curve of the coast could be explained. Most scholars insist that when Fray Marcos said he had heard that the coast turned westward, went "en demanda de ella" (in search of it), and verified that it did indeed do so, he had not time to make an actual trip, but had only inquired about it from the Indians. Others use this statement as proof that Fray Marcos' report was nothing but lies. But Undreiner states that, following the route to the west, the stop where the Franciscan makes this remark was in the Salt River area. From there he could have detoured in the time available to a spot where his view of the mountain ranges might have confirmed the curve of the coastline.

Another argument in favor of the western route was thought to have been found in South Mountain Park's Pima Canyon, on the outskirts of Phoenix. There, a rock may be seen that bears the inscription:

> Fr. Marcos de Niza. Corona todo el nuebo Mexico a su costa. Año de 1539. (Fr. Marcos de Niza. Crown all of New Mexico at his expense. Year of 1539.)

On the assumption that it might be authentic, a protective grill has been placed over it.

Bonaventure Oblasser (Oblasser 1939) bases his theory of a western route, passing near Tucson and Phoenix, on his belief in the authenticity of this inscription. He feels it represented one of Fray Marcos' methods of taking possession of land in the king's name, as the friar says he did at various times.

Certain aspects of the inscription, however, tend to arouse doubt. For example, the wording is suspiciously similar to that found on Inscription Rock at El Morro National Monument, written in 1692 and referring to the Diego de Vargas party returning for the final conquest of New Mexico. In this version it appears incomplete and makes no sense as applied to Fray Marcos' expedition. The Phoenix inscription is discussed in detail by Katherine Bartlett and Harold S. Colton in the April 1940 issue of *Plateau*, published by the Museum of Northern Arizona. Their conclusion is that it was forged, probably in the mid-nineteenth century.

Nevertheless, advocates of the western route theory find support in the fact that Fray Marcos had been ordered by the viceroy to stay close to the coast. Why would he have strayed from it so soon? This could, however, be explained by the receipt of the news concerning the location of the "cities" he was seeking. When Estevan, instructed to scout out the route ahead, sent back word of Indians who had actually seen Cíbola, Marcos may have deviated from his original plan. It would have been natural to follow the trails indicated by his Indian guides, who surely knew the best way to these "cities" which he had told them were the object of his journey.

This could easily have taken him over the route preferred by Bandelier, which was one of the early Indian trade routes, up the Sonora and San Pedro valleys, across the Gila and over the mountains to the Little Colorado drainage and on to Zuñi. This route is probably the most popular with scholars, including Herbert E. Bolton, who also accepts Hawikuh as the final destination.

This explanation could equally well have taken Niza over a route proposed by Charles Di Peso (Di Peso 1974, pp. 75–89), which led into the valley of the Río Bavispe rather than the Río Sonora, on through the area of Clifton and directly into present-day New Mexico. He then would have traveled only slightly east of the state line, along the Blue River and on to Zuñi. Di Peso states that much of this route would also follow ancient Indian trails.

Fray Marcos' route is still uncertain, as are most matters related to his historically important journey. The most extreme view, which some scholars have held, is that Fray Marcos never got to Cíbola at all. Bandelier, who does not subscribe to this theory, considers the Franciscan the most maligned man in history. The severe criticism of Fray Marcos began almost immediately on his return. Cortés claimed that Marcos was merely describing lands of which he himself had advised him. However, Cortés was not an impartial observer. Feeling his authority slipping, he was always ready to claim discovery for himself and was jealous of all other achievements.

The unofficial chronicler of Coronado's expedition, Pedro de Castañeda, made the claim that de Niza had barely reached the area north of the present Arizona border when he received news of Estevan's death, took fright, and turned quickly toward home. However, Castañeda speaks constantly of three priests, as though the friar had companions. Since this seems to be highly inaccurate because neither Marcos nor anyone else mentions any other priests after Brother Onorato was left behind early in the journey, it is hard to believe Castañeda.

Fray Marcos accompanied the Coronado expedition and Castañeda constantly seemed hostile to him and eager to criticize his every move. His statement that the Franciscan had to leave the Coronado company soon after arriving at Cíbola because of the anger of the disillusioned soldiers who found nothing there such as he had reported, is backed up, however, by Coronado's own statement in his letter to the king (Coronado 1864–84). The governor says that the friar had not told the truth in a single thing that he had said, except with regard to the large stone houses. However, Fray Marcos' claims in his *Relación* do not seem so exaggerated as to warrant such accusations. He had been told by Indians that there was gold in Cíbola. In his report, at least, he never claimed to have seen any. His return, as Bandelier has pointed out elsewhere (Bandelier 1887, Part II, Chap. III), may have been due purely to reasons of health.

More contemporary accusers of Fray Marcos are Carl O. Sauer (Sauer 1932, 1937, 1941) and Cleve Hallenback (Hallenback 1949), both of whom have attempted to prove that Fray Marcos could not have made the trip he claimed to have. They have written detailed analyses of his travels in order to show that the timing could not have allowed him to reach Cíbola and return when he did. It is true that there are several inconsistencies in the schedule of his journey, but, since his exact route is still unknown, it seems presumptuous to say that he could not have done it without being certain of just what he did. And so the battle rages on.

By what route, and how far did Fray Marcos go? These are questions that some scholars claim to have answered, but, since others question their claims, the story of de Niza cannot be considered resolved. Bandelier was his staunch defender. Since Bandelier's time new accusers have appeared and other defenders as well. The case is not closed and the issue remains a fascinating one worthy of further attention.

Whatever the true story of Fray Marcos de Niza, he stands as a crucial figure in the Spanish Conquest. He may not have found the anticipated golden cities, he may have been maligned for failing to discover what did not exist, but he did in fact open up hitherto unknown lands. He placed the legend of Cíbola on a more realistic level. He gave Spain a reason to advance and inspired the expedition of Coronado. And though, after that expedition's apparent failure, the dream lay dormant for many years, the seed had been sown for all that followed, from the explorations of Chamuscado, Espejo, Castaño de Sosa and Oñate, to the final reconquest of New Mexico by Diego de Vargas after the Pueblo rebellion of 1680. It all began with Fray Marcos and the slave Estevan who, though neither was a Spaniard, carried the Spanish heritage into the southwestern United States.

How far Fray Marcos went and the route that he followed are less important than the fact that he did go. He discovered new peoples and new places, made contact with new cultures, and thus, for better or for worse, prepared the ground for the development of the West.

Part Two

The Discovery of New Mexico

by the
Franciscan Monk,
Friar Marcos de Niza
in 1539,
by Adolph F. Bandelier

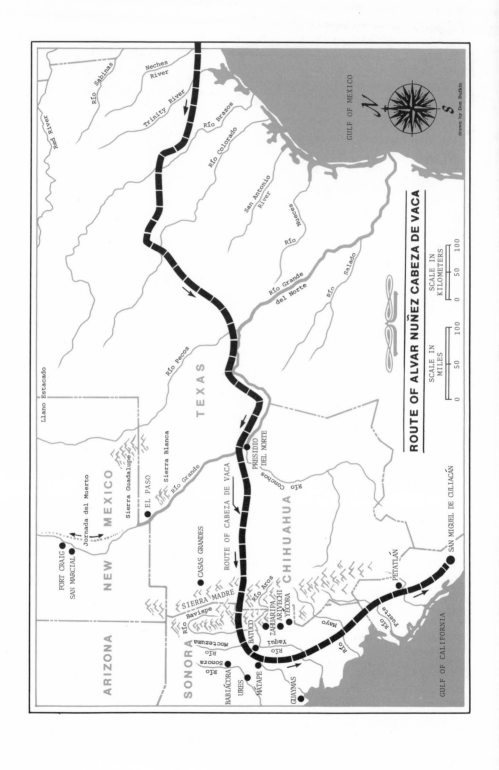

ROUTE OF ALVAR NUÑEZ CABEZA DE VACA

SCALE IN MILES
0   50   100

SCALE IN KILOMETERS
0   50   100

drawn by Don Bufkin

GULF OF MEXICO

Neches River

Trinity River

Río Sabinas

Red River

Río Brazos

Río Colorado

San Antonio River

Río Nueces

Río Grande del Norte

Río Salado

Río Pecos

Llano Estacado

TEXAS

NEW MEXICO

ARIZONA

Sierra Guadalupe

Sierra Blanca

EL PASO

Río Grande

Jornada del Muerto

FORT CRAIG

SAN MARCIAL

ROUTE OF CABEZA DE VACA

PRESIDIO DEL NORTE

Río Conchos

CHIHUAHUA

CASAS GRANDES

SIERRA MADRE

Río Bavispe

Río Aros

ZAHUARIPA

ARIVECHI

YÉCORA

BATUCO

Río Yaqui

Río Moctezuma

Río Sonora

BABIÁCORA

URES

MÁTAPE

GUAYMAS

SONORA

Mayo

Río Fuerte

PETATLÁN

SAN MIGUEL DE CULIACÁN

GULF OF CALIFORNIA

Alvar Núñez Cabeza de Vaca

The original discovery of New Mexico has, up to the present time, been attributed to Alvar Núñez Cabeza de Vaca and his three companions in misfortune, sole survivors of the disaster that struck the expedition of Pánfilo de Narváez* on the Florida and Alabama coasts. This is incorrect; neither did Cabeza de Vaca, nor Alonso del Castillo Maldonado, nor Andrés Dorantes ever set foot in that neo–Mexican land: they had hardly even

---

*Pánfilo de Narváez (1480?–1528), Spanish officer and explorer, played an active part in the early period of the history of the New World. He assisted in the conquest of Cuba in 1511 and, in 1520, was sent to Mexico to arrest Cortés who had displeased the king by exceeding his powers. Unsuccessful in this attempt, Narváez was himself captured by Cortés and imprisoned for two years. Returning finally to Spain, he obtained permission to explore and conquer the lands of Florida. Sailing in 1527, his expedition arrived there the following year and after many hardships, the entire company including Narváez was annihilated except for the four survivors whose saga Bandelier describes. Narváez himself was lost at sea in a fragile boat that had been constructed by the soldiers when their ships were destroyed.

heard of it.* It was their fourth associate, the Negro Estevanico, who first entered a village of sedentary Indians in that portion of what is now the United States of North America, and it was a Franciscan priest, Friar Marcos, a native of Nice[1] who, following the trail of the Negro sent ahead as a scout, brought back to Mexico City the first authentic news of those far-off lands.

In the following pages I shall attempt to demonstrate the truth of these statements, after which I hope to establish what part of New Mexico was visited by these first explorers from beyond the sea.

It is hardly necessary to recall once more that Cabeza de Vaca, treasurer of the ill-fated Narváez expedition, along with Dorantes, Maldonado, and the Negro Estevanico, had alone survived the endless misfortunes that dogged the footsteps of this disastrous enterprise. In about 1529, a year after the other participants had perished, some at the hands of the Indians, some in the frail, hastily built craft in which they had entrusted themselves to a stormy sea that had already engulfed their ships, and some as a result of all manner of privations,[2] these four unfortunates, captives of various native tribes, were reunited by chance in the region bordering on the Gulf of Mexico, probably in western Louisiana. They resolved from that time on never again to separate but to proceed westward as far as possible, to reach the coasts of the Southern Sea (thus was the Pacific Ocean called in those days), where they hoped to find Spanish compatriots. They were exhausted, naked, their bodies bruised and covered with wounds; they possessed not a single weapon. In this state of complete destitution they nevertheless accomplished their purpose in a period of eight years, reaching the little Spanish

---

*Cabeza de Vaca's route from eastern Texas to Culiacán has given rise to another controversy, though not nearly as heated as the one that raged over Friar Marcos' and Coronado's routes. The earlier writers on the subject, Buckingham Smith and W. W. H. Davis, among others, tended to believe that Cabeza de Vaca's party did actually visit the Pueblo Indians in New Mexico. From the descriptions given in de Vaca's *Naufragios,* there seems to be little foundation for this. The nearest thing to a pueblo that he mentions *seeing* is a village of "fixed dwellings of civilization," of which they visited two, but he does not describe them. This was in the area of the "Cow River." (See *Naufragios,* Chapter XXX.) However, there are Indian legends about strange visitors with some vague resemblance to these four travelers.

colony of San Miguel Culiacán (in the present Mexican state of Sinaloa) on May 12, 1536!

Without contemporary documentary evidence showing indisputably, first, that Cabeza de Vaca, as well as his companions, were members of the Narváez armada in 1527 and 1528,[3] and secondly, that they arrived in Culiacán in 1536,[4] there might be a tendency to believe that this extraordinary journey is a piece of fiction, and that the four adventurers were simply impostors. In that case, however, the Spanish government, so cautious, so meticulously scrupulous in all its actions, would not have later rewarded Cabeza de Vaca, and named him governor and adelantado of Paraguay.[5] Then too, as extraordinary as this odyssey may have been in reality, it does not seem at all impossible to one who, though never exposed to conditions as rugged as those that continuously surrounded the four Spaniards for eight years, has nevertheless, upon many occasions, been at the mercy of a variety of perils in lands similar to those through which they traveled in their time.* Indigence, not to say sheer destitution, often arouses the compassion of the most barbarous savage, as well as that of the most depraved of civilized men, and there is nothing attractive about outrageous acts when these can be committed with impunity. Thus, although the journey of Cabeza de Vaca and his friends across the American continent from Florida to the Gulf of California may be an extraordinary accomplishment worthy of admiration, it is nonetheless an historical event that has nothing supernatural or marvelous about it.

To the best of my knowledge, there exists only one separately published account of the vicissitudes of this dramatic episode in the conquest of Spanish America. This account is written by Cabeza de Vaca himself and was printed in Valladolid in 1555. It has, however, three corollaries: one from the lips of the au-

---

*It may seem presumptuous for Bandelier to compare his own travels with those of Cabeza de Vaca, but perhaps justifiable when we consider that Bandelier was not an "outdoorsman" by nature and went through some rather rugged experiences on his journeys in the southwestern area. He traveled on horseback (and even occasionally on foot) through parts of Arizona, Sonora and Chihuahua which were considered unsafe at that time (1883–84) because of Apache depredations. He was once even reported as having been killed by Apaches in Arizona and surprised everyone by riding into Fort Apache safe and sound, whence he hastened to communicate with family and friends by telegraph to report that all was well.

thor, in his conversations with Gonzalo Fernández de Oviedo y Valdés, to which the historian of the Indies devotes one chapter of his great work,[6] and summaries, at least, of two official reports made by the travelers.

Cabeza de Vaca's reports are sometimes precise, but more often they become confused, under the influence of an imagination overstimulated by long suffering. Unfortunately, the points concerning geography and ethnography are sometimes the ones that are treated the most vaguely. The route of the journey is, therefore, subject to interpretations that are mere conjectures, and from this have resulted historical errors that have been perpetuated for several centuries.

It is certain that the point of departure of this journey must have been Florida, then Alabama, and finally Louisiana, west of the mouth of the Mississippi. The fact that this river is not mentioned is only natural; its outlets are many, comparatively narrow, and when crossing them in the delta the true size cannot be estimated as easily as [it might be] in the main stream. Besides, in this area, the Spaniards were wandering, so to speak, from island to island;[7] they were in turn driven forward or forced back by small bands of natives on which they too often bestowed the exaggerated title of tribes.[8]

From the information concerning edible plants that provided the travelers as well as the Indians with food, it is easy to ascertain that, once they reached the mainland, they were in Texas. The principal fruit is the tuna, or Indian fig—in other words, the fruit of the opuntia.[9] Further on he mentions the mezquite (*Algarroba glandulosa*) with its seeds, or rather its edible beans.[10] It would be hopeless to try to fix dates; it is hardly possible to even identify a season of the year.

Nevertheless, we can easily make out the following points. After they left the marshy coasts, the country remained flat for a long time,[11] and there were many deer. The buffalo, or American bison, appeared in the valleys.[12] Finally they caught sight of the mountains which seemed to them to be rising in the direction of the Northern Sea.* They believed that these moun-

---

*The name Northern Sea was given in the sixteenth century to the Atlantic Ocean, which also included the Gulf of Mexico. The Southern Sea, as Bandelier has mentioned, referred to the Pacific Ocean, which also included the Gulf of California.

tains were near the coast, but they preferred to head toward the interior, although continuing to keep to the plains, close to the mountain ranges. However, in spite of their efforts to avoid these sierras, they were obliged to cross part of them.[13] They forded several rivers and complained often about the aridity and desolation of the mountains.[14] To one of these rivers they gave the name Cow River, "because most of the cows* that die are found near there, and because for fifty *leguas* up that river many are killed."[15] Here they came upon the first traces of corn, beans and squash or marrow. The country to the north was described to them as dry and lacking in foodstuffs.[16]

Instead of continuing northward, Cabeza de Vaca and his companions kept to their westerly route, following the river for seventeen days. Crossing this river, they finally came upon dwellings built of earth, as well as of reed matting, in the heart of a very extensive mountain range. The natives had a great deal of corn, cotton fabrics, coral that came from the Pacific Ocean, and lastly, *turquoises.* These turquoises they obtained from the North in exchange for plumes and parrot feathers.[17] All these things were found within a distance of more than a hundred leagues as they continued to travel westward, and the Spaniards finally arrived at a place which they called *Village of the Hearts,* †

---

*These were the American bison that roamed the plains. In many of the ancient documents they are referred to as "humpbacked cows."

†This is the pueblo of Corazones. Coronado passed through it on his way to Cíbola in 1540 and rested there several days. A settlement was established in this spot by Tristán de Arellano, commanding the main body of Coronado's expedition. It was called San Hierónimo de los Corazones and became a sort of way station between Culiacán and Coronado's "colony" in New Mexico. It was soon afterward moved to another site and was destroyed in 1541 by a native uprising, when the Indians took advantage of dissension among the settlers.

The location of Corazones has been the subject of much discussion. It is generally believed to have been situated in the vicinity of Ures on the Río Sonora, though there are tenable arguments that it was, rather, in the upper drainage of the Río Mayo (See Di Peso 1974, IV, p. 64), or even near the Sinaloa-Sonora border, around the present town of Yécora (See Alegre 1956, I, pp. 357–358). Bandelier himself felt that Corazones lay "a short distance from the village of Batuco in Sonora." (See Bandelier 1890a, pp. 64–65.) He points out that "Batuco lies northeast of Guaymas, at a distance of about 110 miles in a straight line." He places Corazones nearer the coast, probably "some place in the vicinity of Mátape," that is, slightly west of the bend of the Yaqui River, not far from the Río Moctezuma.

because of the large number of deer hearts that were offered them to eat. There they found the first signs of the Spaniards and there too they felt assured that they were approaching the Pacific coast.[18] From this spot they apparently turned southward (as I will point out later), encountering their first compatriots near the Río de Petatlán, north of Culiacán in Sinaloa.[19] Badly treated by Diego de Alcaraz, commander of this Spanish outpost, it was not until May 1, 1536 that they were finally turned over to Captain Melchior Díaz, chief alcalde of the province, who tried, by a friendly reception and solicitous care, to make them forget both the vicissitudes of the past and the bad treatment to which Alcaraz, and especially his lieutenant, Cebreros, had subjected them.[20]

Before taking up the subject of the direction and the places indicated by this itinerary, I shall allow myself a few observations concerning the circumstances that made it possible for Cabeza de Vaca and his friends to accomplish the amazing journey that I have just described.

In the travelers' absolutely destitute and defenseless condition, they could only survive with the consent and even the assistance of the Indians. In the beginning the natives held them captive with the purpose of mistreating them.[21] Fleeing to more friendly tribes (or perhaps merely bands), they were obliged to follow the migrations of these nomadic natives. To people who did not cultivate the soil, and consequently had no need of labor, the Christians were quite useless beings. They knew neither how to stalk game, nor to hunt with the bow and arrow; they were ailing and could stand neither the excessive cold, nor the humidity. Such beings remained incomprehensible to the Indians and it is quite natural that the mystery surrounding their situation led the natives to suspect that they were of supernatural origin and talents. They therefore directed them to cure the sick![22] As a last resort, after resisting this strange request for some time, the Christians did the best they could; they imitated what they had seen performed in the presence of the sick by the Indian doctors, adding to this the prayers and symbols of the Christian Church, and this was successful. In a short time they became such famous doctors that, instead of being suffered and tolerated, they were henceforth esteemed and pampered. They took advantage of this ascendancy, not to despoil the natives, but to secure their cooperation in a great undertaking that they were contemplating: that of returning to Mexico by traveling continually westward.[23] From the moment when their reputation as healers of the sick was established, they were the ones who directed the natives' movements; they went from tribe to tribe with no difficulty and always with a following.[24] The Indians obeyed them and led them in the direction that they designated. Already we have here a bit of precious information, for this direction was *that of the setting sun,* and since the native always follows the most direct route possible without being concerned about obstacles that appear insurmountable to us, the result was that Cabeza de Vaca and his companions, once in eastern Texas, traveled almost *directly westward.*

In accordance with the pious attitudes of the period, Cabeza de Vaca attributes the many cures performed by himself and his friends to a miraculous intervention from above. This modest interpretation is no concern of mine at this point. Whatever the general opinion may be about this matter, and although there is practically no doubt that the number of these cures was unintentionally exaggerated, as was the seriousness of the cases in all probability, that is no reason to shrug off in a similar fashion the Spaniards' influential position among the natives as supposed doctors, and the effect of that position on their itinerary.[25] It is easy to become a doctor and a sorcerer among the Indians. Everything that the latter does not understand appears supernatural to him and is derived from a good or evil source which he considers occult. During the five years that I spent among the tribes of the Southwest, both sedentary groups and nomadic Indians, I have often been called upon to help the sick, and the simplest advice, the most minimal remedy that succeeded, immediately attracted to me a clientele that I rid myself of as promptly as possible. For, among the aborigines, between the doctor who heals and the sorcerer who kills (and who is killed in atonement), there is never more than a very small step, in *his* [the Indian's] opinion. An unsuccessful treatment might result in fatal consequences for the one who attempted it.

While keeping in mind the previously mentioned fact that from a certain spot, apparently situated to the west of Louisiana,

Cabeza de Vaca and the others were able to follow in an almost straight line the direction that they chose (thanks to the ascendancy that they had acquired over the natives), and that this direction was regularly a westerly one, if, therefore, we undertake to examine in more detail the route that they may have followed, one thing is certain: the point of departure is located a little to the south of the thirtieth parallel. There lie the coasts, first of Florida, then of Alabama and finally that of Louisiana.[26] Even when they penetrated the interior, it was only to a short distance from the Gulf.[27] It is certain that they did not cross the Mississippi at any point north of the delta, and it is equally certain that they did not reach the Red River (as the Anglo-Americans call it). In the whole area where they were at the time, the "tuna," or fruit of the prickly-pear cactus, constituted the inhabitants' main food.[28] So it was within the quadrangle bounded by the Gulf of Mexico to the south, the Red River to the north, the Mississippi to the east and the Río Sabinas, or perhaps the Trinity River, to the west, that they wandered in the beginning.[29] The latter river is the most likely, and the bison that they saw previously were the forerunners of the immense herds that ranged in those days from the North all the way into Texas. If they had traveled up as far as today's Indian Territory, in other words, north of Texas and east of New Mexico, they would have found a more arboreal vegetation, and more abundant foodstuffs than those that Cabeza de Vaca mentions. Finally, the appearance of mezquite as an edible plant clearly points to Texas! Then too, we must not forget that during this whole period they had the feeling of always remaining near the coast, for when they saw the mountains for the first time, they believed that they sloped down toward the sea and were only fifteen *leguas* from it.[30]

To reach mountains from any part of northern Texas it is necessary, traveling westward, to cross the great dry plains uninhabitable to man. This is especially the case from the Indian Territory, between which and New Mexico lies the Llano Estacado, forming a barrier more than three hundred kilometers wide, without watercourses, without trees, almost without vegetation. And from the western edge of this desert, along the Río Pecos, the Sierra Blanca, which is the nearest mountain range, is still quite far away.[31] Cabeza de Vaca's account, on the other hand, describes a country which Indian tribes, nomadic to some extent within a limited radius, would consider to be consistently suitable for habitation right up to the base of the mountains; such were the Texas tribes. It is in the center of this state, on the other side of the Brazos, that the "Sierras" of the Spanish travelers must be sought, and the river that ran at their base was the southern Colorado. At this point the Indians were already leading them westward according to the Indian custom, in other words, as directly as possible; so the travelers were following approximately the thirtieth parallel. However, they changed direction slightly, following the Brazos upstream for a few days, then crossed over to the Colorado, beyond which, and beyond a plain of thirty *leguas* at least, they came finally upon the Río de las Vacas. This river is the Pecos and the Spaniards reached it very near, if not exactly at, its confluence with the Río Grande del Norte.[32] There is no doubt that this was the Río Pecos, for it is the last place where the bison are mentioned. And indeed this great quadruped has not penetrated (at least not in large herds) farther west than along the banks of this stream, where in times past it was abundant during the hot months.[33]

Here Cabeza de Vaca and the others wanted to go northward up the Pecos, but the Indians dissuaded them. They nevertheless followed a river for seventeen days, after which they crossed it.[34] They had chosen this route "because we were still convinced that by going toward the sunset we would find what we were seeking." So it seems that the river in question led them westward, and this is in fact the case with the Río Grande if, from its confluence with the Pecos, it is followed upstream until it joins the Río Conchos at Presidio del Norte. The great river flows southeast from this spot then turns back up east-northeast, so that its average direction is from west to east. The place where they crossed it must be rather more above the Presidio than below it, for no mention is made after that of any river of much importance. This stream is therefore the last that the Spaniards encountered before entering the "extensive mountains" beyond which lay the Valley of the Hearts. This shows unquestionably that the stream mentioned is the Río Grande!

So, between the Río Grande to the west and the Mississippi

to the east, Cabeza de Vaca had come upon at least four rivers all of which traversed a region that the nomadic Indians found more or less habitable. In this region, the principal native food derived from the vegetable kingdom consisted of the tuna and the mezquite. The forefront of the columns of American bison coming down from the north emerged there. These topographic conditions, these elements of flora as well as of fauna, come together between the two rivers only in Texas, for everywhere else the uninhabited and almost unapproachable plains would not have failed to attract the narrator's attention, and would have considerably modified the route and eventually the result of the journey.

Besides, whatever portion of the Río Grande's course north of Texas Cabeza de Vaca might have touched upon, he would not have failed to hear of the sedentary Indians (Pueblos) of New Mexico. The villages of the latter extended then from Jaos* close to Colorado in the north, to San Marcial or Fort Craig in the south,[35] and all along the river, as well as for a certain distance into the interior on each side. From Fort Craig to the Chihuahua border is barely two hundred kilometers, and this area was ranged by the Apaches, the Mansos and the Zumas, who knew the Pueblos well and who would not have failed to explain to their visitors the unusual architecture of the villages. Finally, it would have been impossible to go up the Río Grande for seventeen days without landing right in the midst of the Pueblos. Cabeza de Vaca not only does not mention them, but he states that the dwellings were of matting and branches.

Thus, I conclude that, during the time that Cabeza de Vaca and his followers remained east of the Río Grande del Norte, they never entered New Mexico territory, but that they crossed the entire breadth of the state of Texas without going up to its northern borders. It is equally certain that during this portion of the journey they heard nothing anywhere about the sedentary Indians of the North, or about their multi-storied houses of stone and sun-dried brick.

---

*This is obviously a misprint for Taos. Since Bandelier's original manuscript is no longer known to exist, only the text of the *Revue d'Ethnographie* is available. The typesetting in this publication was clearly not the best. Also, in Bandelier's handwriting a "T" looks very much like an "I" or a "J," and may have been the source of the error.

It is possible, however, that after crossing the river, and between the latter and the Valley of the Hearts, the Spaniards might have touched upon the Pueblo settlements and that the dwellings of earth, mentioned as having been encountered seventeen days' march from the Río Grande, might have belonged to one or another of their villages.

Pedro de Castañeda, one of Coronado's companions on his expedition to New Mexico, states that Cabeza de Vaca's "Valle de los Corazones" was south of the Valley of Sonora.[36] Coronado, as I believe I have demonstrated elsewhere, entered this valley near Babiácora, that is to say, about two hundred kilometers south of the border that separates Mexico from the North American territory of Arizona.[37] So it is in the state of Sonora, and between the twenty-ninth and the thirtieth parallels, that we should seek the Valley of the Hearts.[38] To reach it from the banks of the Río Grande in the state of Chihuahua, and to pass through the pueblos of New Mexico at the same time, it would be necessary to describe an enormous curve. Cabeza de Vaca states, on the contrary, that they walked westward as directly as possible. But there is even more conclusive proof. The inhabitants of the country where the Spaniards saw the houses of earth, that is to say, very near Corazones, possessed turquoises. They obtained these stones from the North in exchange for *parrot feathers!* There are no parrots in New Mexico, nor even in Arizona; however, their feathers are highly esteemed in the pueblos and are obtained from Sonora and Chihuahua. In these two states and in the great pine forests of the Sierra Madre, which their borders traverse from north to south along the thirtieth parallel, a kind of green and yellow macaw (guacamayos) is fairly common. I have encountered it in the interior of this unexplored mountain range, west of Casas Grandes, where, flitting from tree top to tree top among the tallest firs, it is one of the first to greet the rising sun with its noisy chatter. Thus, in this Sierra Madre, formerly dotted with the small Indian villages of the Opatas, the Jovas, and the Eudeves, whose houses were sometimes of earth,[39] is the place where we should seek the permanent dwellings built of this material mentioned by Cabeza de Vaca, and not in New Mexico, which he neither visited on the west side of the Río Grande, nor to the east of it.

It remains now for us to consider whether the travelers *heard tell* of the neo-Mexican pueblos on their way to Sonora, between the banks of the Río Grande and the Valley of the Hearts; this might seem to be indicated in the following passage:

> They gave us many necklaces and a few pieces of coral which is found in the Southern Sea, and many turquoises that they get from the North; and to me they gave five emeralds shaped into arrowheads, which they use for games and dances, and they told me that they brought them from a very high mountain that lies to the north, and they bought them in exchange for plumes and parrot feathers; they said that there were many people there and very large houses.[40]

The emeralds might well have been green obsidian. There is a great deal of absolutely clear bottle-green obsidian in the Sierra de Huachinera, near the banks of the upper Río Yaqui, in the state of Sonora. This is located north of Batuco (close to the Valley of the Hearts) and about a hundred and twenty-five kilometers away. As for the large houses, it is possible that this was a reference to the tall buildings of the pueblos, but it is equally possible that it may have been a recollection of the adobe villages, then in ruins, that the Northern Pimas inhabited in the old days along the Río Gila in Arizona, and of which the famous Casa Grande is today the best preserved specimen.[41] Until the seventeenth century the Southern Pimas, living quite close to the Valley of the Hearts, occupied similar buildings,[42] and it is not unlikely that they were referring to the dwellings of their brothers to the north, and not to the distant villages of New Mexico.

So, although Cabeza de Vaca can in no way claim the honor of having been the first to discover and visit New Mexico and its inhabitants, it is nonetheless true that his accounts and those of his companions, vague as they may have been, created an impetus in the city of Mexico toward projects of discovery and exploration in the extreme North. New Spain was prepared for expeditions of this sort, for already the fame of *seven cities* said to be rich and populous had been working on the imaginations of the Spanish settlers in Mexico for several years, and attracting the attention of the governors in that direction.

Bandelier's Notes

1.   There are several biographies of Friar Marcos, though abridged. I will mention here: Fray Gerónimo de Mendieta, *Historia eclesiastica Indiana*, published by Don Joaquín García Icazbalceta, in 1870, but written at the end of the sixteenth century; lib. IV, cap. XI, p. 400. "*Natural de la misma Ciudad de Niza, en el ducado de Savoya*" [Ed. note: "Native of the city of Nice in the duchy of Savoy." Although printed in italics, this is not the title of another work, but a quotation from Mendieta in Book IV, Chapter XI, as referred to by Bandelier. The same line is also repeated exactly, except for the words "de Niza" in the references that follow: Book IV, Chapter XLII and Book V, Chapter XLV.] *id.*, cap. XLII, p. 541; lib. V, dec. I, cap. XLV, p. 674; Fray Agustín de Vetancurt, *Menologio franciscano*, reprint of 1871, March 25, p. 117.

2.   Gonzalo Fernández de Oviedo y Valdés, *Historia general y natural de Indias*, vol. III, lib. XXXV, cap. I, p. 582 and reprint of 1853; Antonio de Herrera, *Historia general de los Hechos de los Castellanos en las Islas y la Tierra firme del mar Océano*, dec. IV, lib. II, cap. IV, p. 26, 1726 edition; *ibid.*, lib. IV, cap. VII, pp. 68 and 69; Francisco López de Gómara, *Primera y Segunda Parte de la Historia general de las Indias*, in the *Biblioteca de Autores Españoles*, 1852, by Enrique de Vedia, vol. I, pp. 181 and 182.

3.   *Ibidem.* There is no doubt about this fact, and it would serve no purpose to accumulate evidence.

4.   Without quoting Cabeza de Vaca's account, there is other contemporary evidence. *Première lettre de don Antonio de Mendoza à l'empereur Charles V*, translated by M. H. Ternaux-Compans and published by him in 1838 in the vol. entitled: *Relation du voyage de Cíbola*, in the collection *Voyages, Relations et Mémoires originaux pour servir à l'Histoire de la découverte de l'Amérique;* Herrera, *Historia general*, dec. VI, lib. I, cap. VII, p. 11; Oviedo, *Historia general*, vol. III, lib. XXXV, cap. VI, p. 614; cap. VII, p. 615. The author himself spoke with Cabeza de Vaca.

5.   Oviedo, *Historia general*, vol. II, lib. XXIII, cap. XI, p. 188; Herrera, *Historia general*, dec. VII, lib. II, cap. VIII, p. 35. There is also his own report

on his administration in Paraguay, entitled *Comentarios,* Vedia Collection (vol. I, pp. 549–599), translated into French by M. Ternaux-Compans under the title *Commentaires d'Alvar Nuñez Cabeza de Vaca.* It was in 1540 that the king of Spain named him adelantado of Paraguay. [Ed. note: The title "adelantado" was conferred on an individual responsible for opening up or conquering a new area. He became the military and administrative officer in the newly occupied territory.]

6.   This account [the previously mentioned one by Cabeza de Vaca, himself] was published for the first time in Valladolid, but I quote from the reprint in the Vedia Collection. It bears the title: *Naufragios de Alvar Nuñez Cabeza de Vaca y Relación de la Jornada que hizo a la Florida con el Adelantado Pánfilo de Narváez.* There is a French translation by M. Ternaux-Compans: *Relation et naufrages d'Alvar Nuñez Cabeza de Vaca* (1837). Henceforth I will refer to the Spanish edition simply as *Naufragios,* and to the French translation as *Relation.* The conversation with the author is reported in Oviedo, *Historia general,* vol. III, lib. XXXV, cap. VII, p. 614. According to the same author (*ibid.,* p. 582 and p. 614), the three Spaniards together are said to have made a report to the Royal Audiencia of San-Domingo, "As may be gathered from the account which three gentlemen named Alvar Núñez Cabeza de Vaca, Andrés Dorantes and Alonso del Castillo, who were with the same Pánfilo de Narváez, sent to this Royal Audiencia that sits in this city of Santo Domingo. . . ." [Ed. note: The Royal Audiencia was the supreme governing body in each of the provinces of New Spain. It included the viceroy of the province, but also had jurisdiction over him, since it was responsible only to the Council of the Indies in Spain and to the king himself.] It is from this report that Oviedo borrows what he says about the famous journey. "The chronicler took this account from the letter that these gentlemen sent from the port of Havana, where they put in this past year of 1539, to the Royal Audiencia that sits in this city of Santo Domingo on this island of Española. . . ." So it may be said that we actually have two documents, but Cabeza de Vaca's is the only one that has been published in its entirety and separately. In any case, it seems that there was a third one, according to Herrera, *Hist. general,* dec. VI, lib. I, cap. VII, p. 11: "and they so swore in the town of San Miguel, where they made a statement about it and everything else mentioned here, testifying under oath before a notary on May 15 of this year." It is not impossible that Herrera copied this declaration.

7.   Cabeza de Vaca, *Naufragios,* cap. XII–XVIII, pp. 526–532; Herrera, *Hist. general,* dec. IV, lib. IV, cap. VI, VII, pp. 66–68; Oviedo, *Hist. general,* lib. XXXV, cap. IV, p. 599:

> These people eat nothing but fish during the entire year, and little of that . . . and that is why they move about so often, for if they did not they would have nothing to eat. And in addition to this scarcety, there is another great one, that of fresh water (in which this land is very poor) for, since they travel between coastal swamps and salt water. . . .

8.   The number of tribes mentioned is large. Nevertheless, they had almost nothing to eat! Oviedo, *Hist. general,* vol. III, p. 600: ". . . and most of the year they suffer great hunger, and every day of their lives they have to work from morning till night to satisfy it." Cabeza de Vaca (*Naufragios,* cap. XXVI, p. 537), lists the following languages, corresponding to tribes living, according

to him, between the island that he calls the Island of Mal-Hado, and the place where they began to travel westward: "Caoques, Han, Chorrucos, Doguenes, Mendica, Guevenes, Mariames, Guaycones, Iguaces, Atayos, Acubadaos, Quitoles, Avavares, Malicones, Cutalchiches, Susolas, Comos, Camoles, Higos." Nineteen in all. To date I find it impossible to identify a single name.

9.   Cabeza de Vaca, *Naufragios,* cap. XVIII, p. 532; Oviedo, *Hist. general,* lib. XXXV, cap. IV, p. 601: "These people when summer arrives, at the end of May, eat a certain amount of fish . . . and begin to migrate in order to eat tunas [cactus fruit], which are a fruit very abundant in that country, and they travel for more than forty leagues, as far as Panuco, to eat them. . . ."

10.   *Naufragios,* cap. XXVII, p. 538; Oviedo, *Hist. general,* III, p. 617. He calls it *Mezquizquez.*

11.   Nowhere is there any mention of mountains until the seventh year after the loss of the ships, according to Oviedo, *Hist. general,* lib. XXXV, cap. IV, p. 602.

12.   *Naufragios,* cap. XVIII, p. 52: "And they are accustomed to killing deer by surrounding them with many fires." Oviedo, *Hist. general,* lib. XXXV, cap. IV, p. 601: "and sometimes they kill deer, and it even happens that a few people kill two or three hundred deer. . . . For, since they travel along the coast, the people, forming a line, chase them from the inland side, and since that area remains uninhabited and deserted the entire year, there are a great number. . . ." The bison is mentioned in *Naufragios,* cap. XVIII, p. 532:

> Cows come this far, and I have seen them three times and eaten of them. . . . Of the smaller ones the Indians make cloaks to cover themselves and of the larger ones they make shoes and shields; they come from a great distance to the north, down as far as the Florida coast, and range for more than four hundred leagues over the entire country. . . .

13.   *Naufragios,* cap. XXVII, p. 539; Herrera, *Hist. general,* dec. VI, lib. I, cap. V, p. 8; Oviedo, *Hist. general,* lib. XXXV, cap. V, p. 605.

14.   *Naufragios,* cap. XXVIII-XXX.

15.   *Naufragios,* cap. XXX, p. 542: "and we called them the cow people, because most of those [cows] that die do so near there; and because they [the Indians] go up that river for more than fifty leagues killing great numbers of them." [Ed. note: This passage also appears in the text. The variations in the wording are due to the fact that the version quoted in the text went through the French translation by Ternaux-Compans, used by Bandelier. The translation here is from the original Spanish which is slightly different.]

16.   As far as the details are concerned, there are three different versions here: Cabeza de Vaca, *Naufragios,* cap. XXX, p. 542: "[They told us] that the road followed that river upstream to the north, and that in seventeen days' travel we would find nothing to eat but a fruit called 'chacan'. . . ." Herrera, *Hist. general,* dec. VI, lib. I, cap. VI, p. 9: "They said that up a river to the north they would find many cows for sustenance." Oviedo, *Hist. general,* lib. XXXV, cap. VI, p. 609:

> There they told them that further on there was no more flour, nor beans, nor anything to eat, for thirty or forty days, traveling northward from the direction where the sun sets [i.e., northwest] . . . and that all the Indians there were very hungry, and that they would have to journey upstream in a northerly direction another nine or ten days, without anything to eat. . . .

But the three sources in question agree on the fact that this was where they came upon the first traces of corn. Oviedo is the most explicit (*Hist. general,* III [VI], p. 609: "All the rest [all the other Indians besides those mentioned in the last quotation] had to go westward or toward the setting sun, until they came to a place where there was plenty of corn, and there was also some to the north, on the right hand [i.e., northeast], as well as supposedly further down, throughout the coastal area.

17.   Oviedo, *Hist. general,* III [IV], p. 609: "And these Indians had some small houses of earth built of mud, with flat roofs." *Naufragios,* cap. XXXI, p. 542–543: "Among these houses there were some of earth, and the others were all of reed matting; and from here we traveled more than one hundred land leagues, and continued to find settlements of houses." Oviedo says: "Eighty leagues"; Herrera, *Hist. general (ut supra),* corroborates Cabeza de Vaca or copies him.

18.   *Naufragios,* cap. XXXII, p. 543: "In the village where they gave us the emeralds, they gave Dorantes more than six hundred split deer hearts . . . and for that reason we called it the Village of the Hearts. . . ." Oviedo and Herrera both agree.

19.   *Naufragios,* cap. XXXIII-XXXIV, p. 544 and 545. The two others agree. The place where they encountered Captain Lázaro Cebreros is described as follows by Fray Antonio Tello (*Historia de la Nueva Galicia,* written in 1650, but of which there only remain some fragments published in 1866, in the second volume of *Documentos para la Historia de México,* by my learned friend don Joaquín García Icazbalceta, cap. XII, p. 358): "They were told that the 'conquistadores' were nearby, and following their trail from Yaquimi, in the Ojuelos, one day's journey before reaching Sinaloa, they met Captain Lázaro Cebreros. . . ."

20.   The date is established by Herrera, *Hist. general,* dec. VI, lib. I, cap. VII, p. 11, and by *Naufragios,* cap. XXXVI, p. 546 and 547. The former says: "And after resting there [in San Miguel] fifteen days preparatory to traveling one hundred leagues, which is the distance to the city of Compostela where they found Nuño de Guzmán, who received them very well. . . ." The latter: "And after we had been there fifteen days. . . ."; further on: "We stayed in the town of San Miguel until the fifteenth day of the month of May." So this is old style and we should read May 12 and 27. [Ed. note: According to Bandelier's system of allowing for twelve days' difference between the Julian and Gregorian calendars, May 15 Julian would indeed be May 27 Gregorian. No other date is mentioned in the quotations, so it is not quite clear what May 12 refers to. However, in the portion of the text not quoted by Bandelier, Cabeza de Vaca does say that they arrived in San Miguel on April 1, so perhaps Bandelier meant to say "April 12" instead of "May 12." This would actually be only an eleven-day difference, but it is not unusual for Bandelier to make a slight error of this type in calculation.] As for the bad treatment, this is mentioned in *Naufragios,* cap. XXXIV, p. 545. Cabeza de Vaca is the only one who complains of this. The others, in the account copied by Oviedo (*Hist. general,* lib. XXXV, cap. VI, p. 612), say nothing about it.

21.   Oviedo, *Hist. general,* lib. XXXV, cap. IV, p. 599:

And there they were made slaves and treated more cruelly than by any Moor, for besides going about in this coastal area (which is burning like fire in the summer), with their raw flesh exposed, and entirely naked and unshod, their principal task was to carry on their bare backs burdens of wood and water and everything else that the Indians needed, or to drag canoes through those coastal swamps in that heat.

The Indians made them work like women. (*Naufragios*, cap. XVIII, pp. 531 and 532.)

22. *Naufragios*, cap. XXI, p. 533; Oviedo, *Hist. general*, lib. XXXV, cap. V, p. 603:

And there it was that they first began to fear and respect this handful of Christians and to hold them in esteem. They came up to them and stroked them and stroked themselves, and told the Christians by signs to stroke them and rub them and heal them, and they brought them some sick people so they could cure them, and the Christians did this, although they were more accustomed to working than to performing miracles.

They had already been instructed previously to cure the sick, but they refused. This passage is quite characteristic of the Indians and their type of reasoning (*Naufragios*, cap. XV, p. 528):

On that island of which I spoke they wanted to make us doctors without testing us or asking us for credentials, because they cure sicknesses by blowing upon the sick person, and with that breath and with their hands they cast out illness. They asked us to do the same and to be useful to them in some manner. We laughed at them, saying that it was a joke and that we did not know how to cure anyone; and because of that they took away our food until we did what they told us to. And seeing our obstinacy, an Indian told me that I didn't know what I was saying when I insisted that nothing he knew would succeed, for the stones and other things growing in the field have virtues. He said that he could cure and remove the pain by passing a hot stone over the stomach, and that we who were men certainly had greater virtue and power [than a stone]. Finally, we saw that in such a situation of necessity we had to do it, without anyone sharing the responsibility with us.

This manner of thinking and speaking is very Indian. I myself have often had similar conversations.

23. *Naufragios*, cap. XXI, p. 533: "And afterwards [after three days of celebrations] we asked them about the country ahead, and about the people we would find there, and what sustenance was available there." *id.*, cap. XXVII, p. 538; cap. XXIX, p. 540; cap. XXX, p. 541:

To these people we said that we would like to go toward the setting sun, and they answered that in that direction the inhabitants were far away. We ordered them to send a message to them that we were coming. They excused themselves as best they could ... but they did not dare to act otherwise, and so they sent two women, one of their own and the other a captive of theirs; they sent them because women can negotiate even in time of war ... telling me how frightened they were, begging us not to remain angry, and saying that, although they knew they would die on the way, they would take us where we wanted to go.

24. Oviedo, *Hist. general*, lib. XXXV, cap. V, pp. 606 and 607; *Naufragios*, cap. XXIX, etc. The number is probably exaggerated; however, it is certain that they arrived in Culiacán with several hundred Indians.

25.   *Naufragios,* cap. XV, p. 528:

> What the doctor does is to make incisions where the pain is, and to suck that area. They cauterize with fire, which is a thing that they believe is very advantageous. I have tried it and have had great success with it. And after that, they blow on the place where it hurts, and then they believe that the illness is gone. The way we cured them was by making the sign of the cross over them and blowing on them. . . .

So there were practices that they had learned from the natives, combined with forms of Christian prayer. In addition, they did surgical operations (cap. XXIX, p. 540).

26.   The fact that Narváez landed in Florida does not require substantiation. The spot where he landed was Santa Cruz Bay. The fact that he crossed the southern part of Alabama is revealed in Cabeza de Vaca's report (*Naufragios,* cap. V and VI, pp. 520 and 521; cap. VII and VIII, pp. 522 and 523). Apalache and Aute are places in Alabama. The Bay of Espíritu-Santo, which is mentioned several times in Oviedo (*Hist. general,* III, pp. 592, 593) is one of the branches of the Mississippi estuary, as they also state quite clearly (p. 593): "and for this reason they believed it must be the Río del Espíritu-Santo." The Mississippi was known as the "Río del Espíritu Santo" after 1519, see *Real cédula dando facultad a Francisco de Garay para poblar la provincia de Amichel en la costa firme,* Vol. III of the *Collección de los Viages y Descubrimientos que hicieron por mar los Españoles,* by Martín Fernández de Navarrete, p. 147: "and they crossed a river that they found to be very large and of great volume. . . ." The Spaniards navigated six leagues up this river and the only river in the gulf, except for the Río Grande, that permits such navigation was the Mississippi. This is the opinion of a quite respectable English authority in the Introduction to Volume VIII of the publications of the Hackluyt [sic] Society, entitled *Conquest of Florida by Hernando de Soto, by a gentleman of Elvas* (p. 23). They landed only after passing the Bay of Espíritu-Santo.

27.   Oviedo, *Hist. general,* lib. XXXV, cap. IV, p. 601; cap. V, p. 603.

28.   The evidence is too extensive for there to be any need to point it out.

29.   To reach the Red River they would have had to go north at least 250 kilometers across a swampy and wooded terrain. If the travelers simply skirted the coast of Louisiana and only made a final landing in Texas, it probably was the Trinity. However, I am not myself acquainted with Texas, except for the coasts and the vicinity of El Paso, and therefore I do not presume to make any positive judgment.

30.   *Naufragios,* cap. XXX, p. 541; Oviedo, *Hist. general,* lib. XXXV, cap. V, p. 605: "And then that night they sent down to the sea for people from there, and the following day many men and women came to see these Christians and their miracles . . . and they tried hard to get them down to the sea. . . ." So it seems that they were not far from it. The mountains in Texas are low, and, rather than mountains, are more like high hills outlining plateaus. They are also much farther from the coast than Cabeza de Vaca indicates. But, between the Mississippi and the Río Grande, and even farther on, there are generally no mountains; it is necessary to go much farther, into Tamaulipas, to find any.

31.   There are the Wichita Mountains in Indian Territory, but these are located east of the Llano Estacado. As for the Sierra Blanca, it lies a consider-

able distance from the Pecos. The Sierra Guadalupe is nearer to it, but there still remains the difficulty of crossing the arid desert, which has never been inhabited by Indians, except for nomadic tribes who used dogs to carry their belongings. No mention is made of these dogs, while all the later travelers who visited the plains mention them, beginning with the historians of Coronado's expedition.

32. After crossing this river, they mention no other one the whole time that they traveled westward. Therefore they must have encountered the Pecos near its mouth, for otherwise they would have had to cross the Pecos first, and the Río Grande afterwards.

33. In 1580, as well as in 1583, the Spaniards found large herds of bison in the vicinity of the Pecos. "Testimonio dado en México sobre el descubrimiento doscienta leguas adelante, de las minas de Santa Bárbola governación de Diego de Ibarra." Vol. XV, of the *Colección de Documentos inéditos relativos al Descubrimiento, Conquista y Organización de las antiguas Posesiones españoles en América y Oceania, sacados de los Archivos del Reino, y muy especialemente del de Indias*, p. 149. Antonio de Espejo, *Relación del viage*, vol. XV of the same collection, p. 123: "traveling through it, about thirty leagues for six days [we found] a large number of cows of that region."

34. This is according to the *Naufragios*, cap. XXXI, p. 542. Oviedo, *Hist. general*, III, p. 609, says fifteen.

35. The last ruins showing multi-storied architecture, so characteristic of the pueblos, are located a little to the south of San Marcial in New Mexico. It was there also that Chamuscado, Espejo and Oñate, each in turn, found in 1580 and 1598, the first pueblos of the Piros Indians. Compare also: Fray Alonso de Benavides: *Memorial que Fray Juan de Santander de la orden de San Francisco, comissario general de Indias presenta a la magestad católica del Rey don Felipe Quarto nuestro Señor*, 1630, p. 14. "From this river [Norte] on, the first settlements in the Province and nation of the Piros begin." This was after having passed over the Jornada del Muerto, and the latter ends north of San Marcial or near Fort Craig.

36. Pedro de Castañeda, *Relation du voyage de Cíbola* (P. I, cap. IX, p. 44; P. II, cap. II, p. 157, etc.); Juan Jaramillo, *Relation du voyage fait à la nouvelle Terre*, same volume, pp. 366 and 367 of the appendix.

37. *Cibola*, in the *Sonntagsblatt* of the *New-York Staatszeitung*, May and June, 1885.

38. The Indians who accompanied Cabeza de Vaca were Pimas. They founded Bamoa on the Río de Petatlán. See P. Andrés Pérez de Ribas, *Historia de los Triumphos de nuestra Santa-Fee entre Gentes los mas barbaras y fieras del nuevo Orbe*, etc. Madrid, 1645, lib. I, cap. VII, p. 25. Bamoa is a village in Sinaloa where, according to Manuel Orozco y Berra (*Geográfia de las lenguas y carta Etnográfica de México*, p. 333), the Pima Indians live.

39. If, as I believe, it was south of Casas Grandes (district of Galeana-Chihuahua), that the Spaniards entered the Sierra Madre, they fell among these tribes. According to the *Rudo Ensayo, tentativa de una provincional Descripción geográfica de la Provincia de Sonora, sus Términos y confinantes* (1761–1762), the Jovas occupied, during the last century, Ponida, Joepari, Mochopa, Satechi and the approaches to the Río Mulatos and to the Aros. According to Orozco y Berra, *Geografía, etc.*, p. 345, in 1627 they also lived at Arivechi and at Zahuaripa, while in the seventeenth century the Eudeves occupied, among

other places, Batuco, Bacanora and Mátape (p. 344). Both languages are treated as Opata dialects. See Francisco Pimentel, *Cuadro descriptivo y comparativo de las lenguas indígenas de México*, vol. II, p. 153; *Rudo Ensayo*, cap. V, p. 70, § 1:

> There are two principal nations that populate Sonora, namely the Opatas and the Pimas. I say the principal ones, because the Eudebes and the Jovas may be included among the Opatas, for their language differs as little from Opata as Portuguese does from Castilian or Provençal from French.

40.   *Naufragios*, cap. XXXI, p. 543; Oviedo, *Hist. natural*, III, p. 610, gives a slightly different interpretation.

41.   Casa Grande has been described so often that I will not presume to describe it again here. I visited it in 1883. According to Mr. J. D. Walker, to whom traveling scientists owe so many precious and pleasant memories, this village was built and inhabited by the Pimas. [Ed. note: Judge John D. Walker came to California from Illinois in 1861. He later moved to Arizona and worked at the Pima Agency in Sacaton as a trader and eventually a physician. He served under General Crook as captain of a company of Pima Indians against the Apaches. At one time he was Probate Judge of Pinal County. The Pimas trusted him and made him a councilor in the tribe. He learned both the Pima and Maricopa languages. His hope of writing about his Indian friends collapsed when he lost his mental abilities following a paralytic attack and died in 1891 at the age of 52. Bandelier had visited him at Casa Grande in 1883 and respected him greatly for his deep knowledge of the Pimas.]

42.   Ribas, *Historia de los Triumphos*, etc., lib. VI, cap. II, p. 360, "because they had large adobe walls, made of mud and covered with flat roofs and terraces. They built some of them much larger, and with embrasures like forts. . . ." P. Francisco Javier Alegre, *Historia de la Compañía de Jesús en Nueva España*, vol. I, lib. III, pp. 231–235, is just as explicit.

MOQUI VILLAGES
ZUÑI
ACOMA
RÍO Colorado Chiquito
RÍO Zuñi
EL CARRIZO
ARIZONA
NEW MEXICO
Colorado River
FORT APACHE
Salt River
PHOENIX
Blue River
SAN CARLOS
CLIFTON
Gila River
CASA GRANDE
RIVERSIDE
SAN JOSÉ DEL PUEBLO VIEJO
Santa Cruz River
San Pedro River
FORT GRANT
San Simon Valley
Sierra del Dragón
Papaguería
TUCSON
Sierra Chiricahui
QUITOBAQUITO
EL PASO
Sierra de las Mulas
CHARLESTON
Sierra de San José
Sierra de los Ajos
QUITOVAC
OJO DE AGUA DEL VALLE
FRONTERAS
GULF OF CALIFORNIA
ALTAR
MUTUTICACHI
CASAS GRANDES
BACUACHI
RÍO Bavispe
SIERRA MADRE
SONORA
CHIHUAHUA
BANÁMICHI
RÍO Moctezuma
BACERAC
HUACHINERA
RÍO Sonora
SÁTACHI
URES
MOCHAPA
HERMOSILLO
TEÓPARE
Tiburón Island
MÁTAPE
RÍO
ZAHUARIPA
RÍO Aros
ARIVECHI
RÍO Mátape
YÉCORA
GUAYMAS
ROUTE OF MARCOS DE NIZA
RÍO Yaqui
BAJA CALIFORNIA
RÍO
RÍO Mayo
RÍO Fuerte
Petatlán
PETATLÁN
BAMOA
RÍO

**ROUTE OF
FRIAR MARCOS DE NIZA**

SCALE IN MILES
0   50   100

0   50   100
SCALE IN KILOMETERS

N
S

drawn by Don Bufkin

SAN MIGUEL DE CULIACÁN

Fray Marcos de Niza

The legend of the seven cities is an ancient one. It is to be found, among other places, on the *Universalior Cogniti Orbis Tabula* of Jan Ruysch, of the year 1508.* This legend tells the story of the flight of a Portuguese bishop to an island called Antilia, with a number of Christians whom the Moors had driven out of the Iberian peninsula.[1] Around the year 1529 Nuño de Guzmán, then president of the Royal Audiencia of Mexico, governor of New Galicia, but in actual fact of the whole of New Spain, was told, so the story goes, by an Indian from Oxitipar, that to the north lay seven cities "so large that they could be compared to Mexico City and its suburbs." To reach them it was necessary "to penetrate the interior, heading northward between two

---

*Jan Ruysch was a German geographer who accompanied various voyages of exploration from the northern coast of England to the north and west. It is possible that he sailed with the Cabots to the New World. Ruysch's map was published in the Roman Ptolomy of 1508 and was the first known engraved map showing discoveries in the West. It indicates a large island called Antilia about half way between the Azores and the Caribbean islands, among which Hispaniola in particular is identified (see Winsor 1886).

seas."[2] This tale, preceded by that of the Amazons,* which had already prompted Cortés to undertake explorations in the direction of Xalisco, led Nuño de Guzmán as far as Sinaloa. His scouts even reached the southern part of the state of Sonora. There, on the banks of the Río Yaqui, two of his officers, Alcaraz and Cebreros, obtained details that were even more confused concerning the northern lands.[3] Thus, they were told of a great river, which the people along its banks had barred by means of an iron chain! The fall of Guzmán in 1536, well deserved in any case, threw all efforts in that direction into confusion; his successor, Diego de Torres, died in 1538,[4] before he had the chance to concern himself with discoveries, and Francisco Vásquez Coronado, son-in-law of Treasurer Alonzo de Estrada, was only confirmed as governor of New Galicia on April 18, 1539.[5] Three years had elapsed since the arrival of Alvar Núñez Cabeza de Vaca and his companions in Culiacán; however, nothing had been done. And indeed, it was no lack of energy or wisdom on the part of the men who governed New Spain in those days that caused this apparent inertia. The temporal authority, wielded in the name of the Crown by Don Antonio de Mendoza, was supported by Pedro de Alvarado, and Cortés himself appeared on the surface to be on good terms with it at that time. In conjunction with a church from which echoed the great names of Fray Martín de Valencia,† Fray Toribio de

---

*The tale of the Amazons had been circulating in the New World for some time and was said to have been brought there by Columbus himself. It claimed that, on an island named Matenin, at first supposed to be in the Caribbean, lived · a warlike race of women who wore copper armor like the Amazons of ancient legend. The locale of the story was transferred to the mainland, and in Cortés' time the island was presumed to be off the west coast of Mexico.

†Martín de Valencia (1474?–1554), Franciscan missionary from Valencia in Spain. Agustín de Vetancurt in his *Menologio Franciscano* gives his real name as Martín de Buil. He entered the order at the Convent of Mayorga and went first to Portugal. He embarked for the New World in 1524 as superior of the twelve first friars who accompanied the Conquest. He was much given to visions and was said to have performed miracles. His life was very strict and ascetic. Though he never learned the Indian languages, his manner of living was an example to all and his baptisms many. Predicting his own end, he died beneath a tree on the way to Mexico City from Tlalmanalco in the year 1554.

Paredes (nicknamed Motolinía),* Archbishop Zumárraga,† the Bishop of Chiapas, Fray Bartolomé de Las Casas,‡ Fray Luis Cancer,§ Fray Pedro de Angulo,‖ it lacked neither the intellec-

---

*Toribio de Paredes (Motolinía) (?–1569). He came from the town of Benavente in Zamora, Spain and thus is often called Toribio de Benavente. He was best known, however, as "Motolinía," which meant "poor" or "humble" in Nahuatl. It was said that this was the first Nahuatl word that he learned and he felt it suited him. He was one of the first group of twelve friars who came to the New World in 1524. A defender of the Indians, he traveled throughout Mexico and as far as Guatemala. He was one of the founders of the city of Puebla. Motolinía is especially known for his *Historia de los Indios de la Nueva España*. He died in Mexico City, the last of the famous twelve.

†Juan de Zumárraga (1468–1548), first bishop of Mexico and member of the Franciscan order. He championed the rights of the Indians, but his action in burning collections of ancient Aztec manuscripts to destroy all traces of non-Christian religion became quite controversial. In 1546 he was raised to Archbishop. He was instrumental in founding several major schools for the Indians and established a hospital in Mexico City. He was responsible for the introduction of the first printing press into the New World.

‡Bartolomé de Las Casas (1474–1566) came to America in 1502 as a settler on the Island of Hispaniola. He became a priest in 1510, the first to be ordained in the New World, and entered the Dominican Order. He established himself as the champion of the Indians and was later called the "Apostle of the Indies." His defense of the Indians' rights became extremely controversial and he was accused of having started the "leyenda negra" which painted the Spaniards as cruel and unjust toward the natives. Las Casas preached against the "encomienda" system which subjected Indians to Spanish land-holders in return for protection. He felt this was nothing more than a type of slavery, and was instrumental in the passage of new laws to protect the Indians. He was Bishop of Chiapas from 1544 to 1547. He is best known for his *Brevissima relación de la destrucción de las Indias* and for his *Historia general de las Indias*.

§Luis Cancer was probably born in the last decade of the fifteenth century, near Zaragoza, Spain. He arrived in Santo Domingo in 1517 as an ordained Dominican. He spent twenty-three years there and in other parts of the Caribbean. He founded the first *convento* of San Juan in Puerto Rico and stayed there until about 1538. Cancer came to Mexico with Las Casas in 1546. It is said that, once, returning to Spain, he was captured by Saracens and ransomed by a French merchant. He worked with Las Casas and Pedro de Angulo in the attempt to conquer a portion of Guatemala by peaceful means. In 1549, he was killed in Florida by the Indians near Tampa Bay.

‖Pedro de Angulo (ca. 1500–1561) came from a noble family of Burgos. He went to the New World as a soldier in 1524 and took part in the later events of the Conquest. He joined the Dominicans in Mexico and founded several *conventos*, or priests' houses. He became a companion of Las Casas and worked with him mainly in Guatemala, where he assisted him in attempting a peaceful conquest of the province of Tezulutlan. De Angulo was named Bishop of Vera-Paz in 1559, but died before assuming his position.

tual strength nor the moral support to attempt great things. But what it did lack was, primarily, the material means, and secondly, the unity indispensable to any external action. It is true that, after the Conquest, Mexico had not had to go through the bloody disturbances to which Peru fell prey at that time, but all the caution and firmness of the Spanish government had been required to avoid similar disasters. First of all, Cortés had to be removed, for he threatened to become a far more dangerous enemy than Gonzalo Pizarro* had ever been in Peru. Next, the disorders provoked by the administrators who were to replace Cortés had to be suppressed. Then, after setting up the government of New Galicia as a barrier to Cortés' encroachments in the North, the first leader to whom this new province was entrusted, Nuño de Guzmán, had to be firmly punished for his criminal conduct toward the Indians, as well as toward his own compatriots. So Viceroy Don Antonio de Mendoza's task consisted in a complete reorganization of the vast and heterogeneous empire that had been placed in his care, and altogether it was a slow, difficult and painful one.

In spite of that, the viceroy did not forget the perspectives that the accounts of Cabeza de Vaca opened up into the interior and beyond the known frontier. It seems that already in 1538, two priests, Fathers Fray Juan de la Asunción and Fray Pedro Nadal, left on January 31 and traveled northeast about six hun-

---

*Gonzalo Pizarro (1506?–1548) was one of Francisco Pizarro's three half brothers who accompanied him to Peru. He was a bold adventurer with many exploits to his credit. After Francisco was killed, Gonzalo felt it incumbent upon himself to obtain the leadership of Peru. This he did through the support of the populace which was rebelling against the new laws imposed by the Crown granting freedom to the Indians and curtailing the privileges of the Spaniards. Defeating Francisco's successor, Vaca de Castro, and the appointed viceroy, Blasco Nuñez Vela, Gonzalo became governor and captain-general of Peru. He soon, however, let his power go to his head and challenged the authority of the king himself. He was ultimately defeated by the forces of Pedro de la Gasca, envoy of the Crown, sent to Peru to regain control for the king. Gonzalo was captured and beheaded in 1548.

Cortés may have had the potential to become more dangerous than Gonzalo, and was probably a more intelligent man, but he never actually regained power once the Conquest was secured. His threat arose mainly from his constant machinations and his attempts to mount expeditions that would again place him in a position of prominence.

dred *leguas*, as far as the banks of a great river that they were unable to cross; this forced them to retrace their steps. This river, according to Fray Nadal's astronomical observations (necessarily quite incomplete), was situated on the 35th parallel, and the source from which I draw this information identifies this river as the one that is now the Gila! So these two priests would have been the first white men to have set foot on the soil of southern Arizona. Their expedition was undertaken by order of Viceroy Mendoza.[6]

In those days, the religious were powerful auxiliaries of the Spanish government in anything involving difficult and hazardous explorations. They were at the same time inexpensive auxiliaries, for their journeys, undertaken with the most limited means, were journeys with a mission and were, consequently, the responsibility of the orders to which they belonged. After the fruitless attempt of the year 1538, Don Antonio de Mendoza did not become discouraged, and since the Franciscans were most widespread in the northern part of New Spain, he immediately consulted with their provincial, who was then Fray Antonio de Ciudad-Rodrigo. To undertake a new journey to the north the latter chose Fray Marcos, a native of Nice, and consequently referred to as *Fray Marcos de Niza* in Spanish sources. He was a "regular priest, pious, endowed with all virtues and dedication," and who was "approved and recognized as capable of making this journey of discovery, not only because of the qualities indicated above, but also because of his knowledge of theology, and even of cosmography and navigation."[7]

Fray Marcos was no novice among the difficult American missions. Having arrived in Mexico in 1531, he went almost immediately to the Pacific coast, and from there to Peru the following year, and accompanied Sebastian de Belalcázar to Quito. Returning to Mexico (probably with Pedro de Alvarado), he made a name for himself because of the qualities that I have just mentioned, as well as through his writings.[8] So the choice appeared to be a happy one.

In order to be sure that the missionary had a useful companion, the viceroy assigned to him, as a guide placed under his orders, the Negro Estevanico who had accompanied Cabeza de Vaca and who, consequently, was acquainted with some of the country and knew, or believed he knew, how to handle the savage tribes. In addition, six Indians, natives of Sinaloa, to whom, in Mexico City, Father Marcos had given some instruction in the Spanish language as well as in religion, were assigned to accompany him. Together with Francisco Vásquez Coronado, who was about to take over the government of Culiacán and the whole of New Galicia, the Franciscan friar left the city of Mexico in the fall of the year 1538. On November 25 (old style),* he acknowledged receipt, probably in the city of Culiacán, of the written instructions from the viceroy that Coronado had just transmitted to him.[9]

These instructions bear witness both to a feeling for justice and humanity, and to a great deal of circumspection on the part of Don Antonio de Mendoza. He begins by enjoining the missionary:

> First, as soon as you arrive in the province of Culiacán, you are to exhort and encourage the Spaniards who live in the city of San Miguel to give good treatment to the Indians who are at peace with us, and not to employ them for excessively hard labor. You are to assure them that, if they act thus, favors of all sorts will be granted them and His Majesty will provide them with compensation for the ills that they have suffered. They will find in me a person who will give them strong assistance in so doing; but if they conduct themselves otherwise, they will be punished and will receive no mercy. You are to inform the Indians that I am sending you in His Majesty's name to request that they be well treated. You will tell them that the Emperor had been very concerned about the ills that they have been made to suffer, that henceforward things will be different, and that anyone who mistreats them shall be punished.
>
> You are to assure them that they will no longer be forced into slavery, that they will no longer be taken from their land, and that, on the contrary, they will be allowed to live in their homes

---

*This refers to the Julian Calendar which was still in effect at the time when these events were taking place. However, by then the spring equinox was found to have been thrown back by roughly 10 days. Ever since the Council of Nicaea in 325, efforts had been made to solve the problem but no satisfactory correction was adopted until 1582 when the new Gregorian Calendar announced by Pope Gregory XIII went into effect. This reestablished the equinox on March 21 and set the year at 365 days, with an extra day every four years, except when this fell on a century year not divisible by 400. Thus, a century year would only be a leap year every four centuries.

in freedom without any harm or wrong being done them. See
that they banish all fear. . . .

After informing the priest that the Negro is being assigned
to him as a guide and that the latter is to "obey him in all things,
as he would myself," and that, in addition, the governor, "Francisco Vásquez, will engage in the same manner the Indians who
came with Dorantes and the other natives of this region who
may be available, so that if you believe, you and the governor,
that you should take them with you, you may do so . . . ," the
viceroy makes the following recommendations to him concerning the journey itself:

> You will always try to travel as safely as possible. First of all, you
> will find out whether the natives are at war among themselves;
> you will avoid giving them any cause to take action against your
> person, which would make it necessary to move against them and
> punish them, for, in that case, instead of going there to do them
> good and to enlighten them, the opposite would take place.
>
> You will take great care to note the strength of the tribes,
> whether they are numerous or not, whether they live scattered
> or together; the appearance and fertility of the country, the
> temperature, the trees, the plants, the wild animals that are to be
> found there; the nature of the soil, whether it is dry or traversed
> by rivers, whether these are large or small; the rocks and the
> metals that it contains. If you can obtain samples of all these
> objects, bring them with you or send some back, so that His
> Majesty may be fully informed.
>
> Inquire continually if anyone has any knowledge of the proxim-
> ity of either the Northern or the Southern Sea, for it is possible
> that there might be a gulf through which the sea penetrates the
> interior. If you reach the coast of the Southern Sea, you are to
> bury on the shore, at the foot of a tall and prominent tree, letters
> in which you will give an account of anything you might feel
> it useful to make known. So that the tree where you leave the
> letters may be identified, you will make a cross upon it, as well
> as at the mouth of rivers, in places that might serve as ports, and
> you will deposit letters there. If ships are sent, they will have
> orders to look for this sign.
>
> You will not fail to see that Indians are continually dispatched
> to report on the route that you are taking, how you are received,
> and what you find that is most remarkable.[10]

Thus equipped, prepared and escorted, Fray Marcos de Niza
left Culiacán with the Negro and a lay brother named Onorato,

on Friday, March 7/19, 1539.* They were traveling north-ward.[11]

Arriving at the banks of the Pitatlán [or Petatlán] River, they stopped, probably in the village of Bamoa. The Indians who live there speak the language of the Lower Pimas of Sonora. It was then a recently established colony, having been founded only two years before by the Indians who had followed Cabeza de Vaca from the Valley of the Hearts and its vicinity. Here, Brother Onorato fell ill, and it was necessary to leave him there and continue without him, after resting three days in the village of Pitatlán.[12] Everywhere the Indians received them in the friendliest manner, though they were frightened "by the Christians of the city of San Miguel who, until that time, had been accustomed to making war upon them and reducing them to slavery."[13] Since the distance that they had then covered was according to Fray Marcos' calculations, "between twenty-five and thirty leagues beyond Pitatlán," it follows that the natives of the country spoke a dialect of the Cáhita or Yaqui language.[14] It was not difficult for the missionary to make them understand him through the Indian interpreters who accompanied him, for the latter were either the nearest neighbors of these natives, or were themselves of the same people. The road probably did not lie far from the coast, for they were in constant communication with its inhabitants. Four days' journey beyond, after crossing a desert (*desierto*, in the sense of an uninhabited country, and not designating a dry and sandy region), they fell among Indians who had no knowledge of white men. These Indians gave them to understand through interpreters that in the interior "four or five days' travel from the place where the mountain ranges end, in a very broad plain, there are a considerable number of large cities inhabited by people who wear cotton." What they gave him to understand besides, concerning the knowledge that these people were said to have of gold and the use they made of it, is subject to question. The friar showed them the metals that he

---

*Bandelier's two dates represent the Julian and Gregorian calendars (see previous note). The difference should actually be 9 or 10 days in 1539, not 12, as this difference increases a little over one day per century and was about 10 days in 1582 when the Gregorian Calendar was installed. Bandelier is quoting the difference more nearly as it would be in his time.

carried in order to learn about those of the country; "they took the gold and told me that these natives had basins of this material, and that they wore round objects of gold in the nose and ears; that they had little scoops of the same metal with which they scraped away the sweat to rid themselves of it."[15] Then he adds the following observation which is of great importance in determining the route that the missionary followed: "But since this plain turns away from the coast, and since my intention was not to stray far from it, I resolved to leave it for my return in order to observe it better."

The Mayo Indians (a branch of the Yaqui), among whom, or very close to whom, Fray Marcos found himself, had no knowledge then of any metals whatsoever.[16] Those that the friar showed them, they judged and compared with known materials according to their *external appearance* only, and not according to their physical characteristics. Gold was yellow; they concluded quite naturally that the yellowish pottery of the Pimas, and the yellow ornaments that they wore, were of the same substance. Also, gold resembled the color of this pottery[17] more than did red copper, bluish iron, tin, bronze, or even brass. As for the priest, who had been in Peru where the natives possessed golden utensils, when he heard tell of rather large settlements, saw nothing extraordinary in the conclusion to which the Indians' response led him: that these peoples had vases and other objects of the same metal. It was a misunderstanding, but all the more inevitable since they understood each other's words without suspecting the great divergence that lay in their points of view.

It was from the Mayos or the Yaquis that the Franciscan received this information. The larger populations which he was told were living in the interior, were evidently the Pimas of Sonora, who occupied and still occupy in part the region around the western slopes of the Sierra Madre, between the twenty-eighth and the twenty-ninth parallels.

From the Mayos or Yaquis he passed on to Vacapa. The word would indicate that it belongs to the Pima language which is also called Névome, and Friar Marcos tells us that the place was "forty *leguas*" from the sea. So he was beginning to turn away from the coast and to head more toward the north-northeast. On the map drawn up by the Jesuit father Eusebius Kühne (Eusebio Kino) we find *St. Ludov. de Bacapa,* but this mission is situated almost west of the city of Tucson, in Arizona.*[18] Leaving Culiacán on March 19, Fray Marcos arrived in Vacapa two days before Passion Sunday,†[19] and in such a short time he would hardly have been able to travel farther than central Sonora. The idea expressed to me last year by a person whose opinions I have always found interesting and most useful, Don Epitacio Paredes of Magdalena in Sonora, that Vacapa was then located not far from the mission of Mátape[20] (formerly Matapa), is therefore not unlikely. However, Mátape is classified as a village of the "Eudeves" by Don Manuel Orozco y Berra, but in any case it lay at the outer confines of territories covered by the Pima and Opata languages, and Eudeve is a dialect of the latter.

On the afternoon of Passion Sunday Fray Marcos sent the Negro Estevanico ahead with some Indians to reconnoiter the country. He had also previously sent Indian messengers toward the sea by three different routes so as to obtain information about the coast. The Negro, on the other hand, was to advance about fifty or sixty leagues northward to see whether in that direction,

> ...he could discover anything important related to what we were seeking. I arranged with him that if he learned there were populated, rich and sizeable countries there, he would no longer proceed, but would return in person or send Indians bearing a sign that we had agreed upon. If it was a country of ordinary size, he was to send me a white cross a span in height; if it was larger, the cross was to be of two spans, and if it was larger than New Spain, the sign was a large cross.[21]

---

*This is not quite accurate. Kino's Bacapa was actually more southwest of Tucson, possibly in the vicinity of the modern village of Quitovac in Sonora. Bandelier may have been confusing this with Quitobaquito in Arizona, a location now within Organ Pipe Cactus National Monument, but which was still sparsely settled in Bandelier's time.

†Passion Sunday in the ecclesiastical calendar is on the second Sunday before Easter. In 1539 it fell on March 23 (Julian Calendar), since Easter was on April 6.

Friar Marcos only moved away from the coast reluctantly, and
in this he was directly obeying the instructions of Viceroy
Mendoza.

He was more than a little surprised when, only four days after
Estevanico's departure, natives whom the latter had sent him
arrived with a cross the size of a man and with the request that

> ... he follow immediately, saying that he had found people
> who told him of the largest country in the world, and that he had
> with him Indians who had been there; he was sending me one of
> them. He sent me word of such surprising things concerning his
> discovery that I refused to believe them before having seen
> them myself.

So he questioned the Indian, whom he found very intelligent,
and the latter told him

> ... that it was thirty days' travel from the place where Estevan
> was to the first city of the country called Cíbola.... He states
> positively and assures me that in this first province there are seven
> very large cities all of which belong to one ruler. Large houses
> of stone and lime are to be found there; the smallest are of one
> story surmounted by a terrace; there are some of two and three
> stories. That of the ruler has four, very well laid out. At the doors
> of the main houses many turquoise ornaments are to be found,
> which stones are very common in the area. The inhabitants of
> these cities are very well dressed. He gave me many other details
> concerning these seven cities and other more distant and larger
> provinces than that of the seven cities.[22]

Although in a hurry to follow the Negro's trail, Fray Marcos
had to await the return of the messengers whom he had sent to
the coast, and they did in fact return on Easter Sunday. Their
accounts were not encouraging; these coasts were poor as were
the neighboring islands. Their inhabitants (apparently the
Seris),[23] who returned with the messengers, brought him "very
well made shields of cowhide, large enough to reach from head
to foot; there are openings made above the place where the
handle is affixed so that it is possible to see from behind. They
are so strong that I do not believe that a shot from a harquebus
could penetrate them." What the Franciscan here takes to be
shields of bison hide were in all probability made from the skin
of the large red or brown deer (*Cervus canadensis*), which ranged

south as far as the mountainous sections of northern Sonora. This magnificent animal stands almost as high as the domestic ox. By a strange coincidence, on the same day arrived "three Indians of the race known as the Painted Ones. Their faces, chests and arms were painted; they live to the east. A certain number live in the neighborhood of the seven cities." These natives were Pimas.[24]

Thinking that Estevanico was waiting for him along the road as had been agreed, the priest set out to overtake him and left Vacapa in the morning, the second day after Easter. He had with him, among others, two Seris from Tiburón Island and three Pimas from the east. But Estevan did not wait for him; he continued on his way, content to send messengers to his superior from time to time with crosses of a size equal to that of the first. Castañeda says: "He thought he could obtain the greatest honor for himself by going alone in search of such famous cities";[25] this is possible, but his ambition cost him most dearly later on.

In order to form an idea of the route that the friar, as well as the Negro, was following, we must first of all remember that they were traveling toward the *north*, and also that Indians *who knew the country* were guiding them *willingly*, therefore, by the most direct routes possible. This route was a known one and, though it was not a road in our present sense of the word, there were nevertheless regular communications at short intervals between Cíbola and the interior of Sonora. When, two days after that of his departure, Fray Marcos reached the place where he expected to find Estevanico, he received even more precise information from the inhabitants; they told him "that they visited the first city called Cíbola, and that they were employed there for digging and for other tasks; that the inhabitants gave them cowhides and turquoises in payment; that all the people of that city wore fine, beautiful turquoises in their ears and noses."[26] Besides the information that he had obtained at Vacapa, he was told that the people of Cíbola were clothed in cotton, that they wore turquoise belts, cloaks and well-worked cowhides. Besides Cíbola there were three other kingdoms called Marata, Acus and Totonteac.[27]

Regular trade relations existed between Sonora and the Indians of the New Mexican pueblos as late as 1859.[28] The latter came in caravans in the month of October, bringing the products of their industry and buffalo hides. They exchanged them for local merchandise, parrot feathers, coral and shells from the coasts. At the present time, when the Pueblos of the Río Grande, as well as those of Zuñi, are asked the source of the materials of which their most sacred ornaments are made, they answer briefly: *Puerto de Guaymas.* Many of these objects are quite old and date from a very remote period. So there was an ancient trade between the North and the South. It was of modest proportions and not at all as magnificent as we have often been led to believe, for where there is no money there is little opulence. This trade or traffic takes place and has taken place since time immemorial, even between enemy tribes, and thus it is that objects originating in the North, the South, the West or the East were able to pass gradually and by degrees from hand to hand to the opposite ends of the continent. War facilitated these movements; when a village was surprised and razed, unfamiliar and striking objects were picked up, they were preserved at first as souvenirs, then as relics and finally as objects of worship. But along with these objects, trade and war transmitted geographical and ethnographical knowledge in the same way. The existence of the Mississippi was known in Pecos,[29] because the great uninhabited plains that lay a few days away from this ancient pueblo became—thanks to the buffalo hunt to which the Indians of Arkansas, as well as those of the Río Grande, went periodically—an exchange where news from one half of the continent was traded for that from the other. This news, entrusted only to memory, became distorted with time, and local names, especially, often became unrecognizable.

Thus it has been impossible, up to the present time, for me to find the word Cíbola referring to any particular locality. There is in the Opata language *Ci-vo-na-ro-co;* but this name is applied to a very dangerous trail along the sides of a rock that abuts the upper Río Yaqui east of Huachinera. It means: the rock where a detour is made (*el peñasco en donde rodean*). The Pimas of Arizona call the ruin known as Casa Grande on the Río Gila, northwest of Tucson, *Ci-vano-Qi* (the house of Civano), but this locality cannot be considered because it is northwest of central Sonora, too close to fit into Father Marcos' route, and because, according to Pima tradition, its houses were already abandoned in the sixteenth century. Besides, according to the accounts of Coronado's subsequent expedition, Cíbola was a *cold* country,[30] while Casa Grande has literally a torrid climate. The word Cíbola must therefore have been borrowed from a language other than those of Sonora or southern Arizona.

If it is a fact that the inhabitants of the place from which the Negro had sent Friar Marcos the first news of Cíbola went there to *work*, then these Indians were sedentary in their own country. In that case, they were Opatas, or Joyl-ra-ua, for the Seris would not have agreed to such service. Three days' journey to the north of Mátape brought the traveler into the valley of the Río Sonora near Banámichi, well populated (relatively) then as now. But it is also possible that he bore more to the west. In any case, he traveled beyond Vacapa for five days, from village to village, received everywhere with great consideration, feasted and pampered, and finding, at almost every stopping point, crosses set up by Estevanico as signs of encouragement. All the inhabitants wore turquoises and they had so-called cowhides in abundance. All spoke of Cíbola as a place well known to them.[31] There is certainly some exaggeration when the missionary refers to these objects in such terms. It is very possible, even probable, that the inhabitants of Sonora had bison hides, but certainly not in such considerable quantities. The same is true of the turquoises. However, everything indicates a sedentary and trading population, to the extent that the Indians were able to be, and this fits the Opatas of the Río Sonora better than the inhabitants of any other northern section of that state. Consequently, I. favor the route up the above-mentioned river and up the valley that it follows as being the one that the Franciscan took. At the end of this inhabited area he came upon a desert that required four days to cross; not an arid plain such as is customarily meant by this word, but simply a region where nobody lived. These deserts were well known in America in those days for they separated the independent enemy tribes like so much neutral ground.[32]

In the situation that we have supposed, it is at Bacuachi, or perhaps four *leguas* to the north, at Mututicachi, that we should look for the end of the inhabited valley.[33] In these villages he received new details concerning the North; he heard tell that at Totonteac they wore clothing of a grayish material that resembled that of which the priest's habit was made. He was told that in the place referred to there were small animals that furnished the material for this cloth and that they were the size of the two greyhounds that Estevan was leading with him.[34]

It seems too that there Friar Marcos took a side trip toward the coast and assured himself that, at a latitude of about thirty-five degrees, it turns west.[35] It is rather far from Bacuachi to the gulf coast, but it is certain that at that latitude it does take a very definite turn toward the northwest. As for the astronomical position, it is quite incorrect, but there is nothing surprising in that, nor is it anything for which to reproach him, in view of the state of knowledge and the instruments of the period.

The four-day desert, which the friar then had to cross is, in all probability, the mountainous country between Bacuachi and the present Arizona border. North of Mututicachi the little Río Sonora emerges from a long narrow gorge, which does not leave much space for the dwellings of agricultural Indians. One might say that, from its source in the Ojo de Agua del Valle to this outlet, over a distance of nearly sixty kilometers, there are only three places, Los Fresnos, Cañada Ancha and Janover-Achi, which offer space at all suitable for village sites. Indeed, I have found only a few Indian ruins there, and those that exist are almost obliterated. They give the impression of having been abandoned for many centuries.

If, instead of following the course of the river upstream, the Franciscan headed directly north, he must have found a complete and nearly inaccessible desert. There, he must have encountered mountains such as the Sierra de San José, the Sierra de los Ajos, which delayed his progress, forcing even the Indians to make detours. If we now take a look at the region more to the west, it presents even more formidable obstacles. Emerging from the mountains of Sonoytac or Altar, the desert of Papaguería, dry, barren, fearfully hot, stretched between him and the Río Gila, and to cross this area throughout which the most savage branch of the great family of the Upper Pimas then ranged, the months of May and June were the most favorable ones. To find a route, there is hardly any choice except between the Santa Cruz valley to the east and that of the San Pedro to the west;* leaving Sonora[36] after crossing the desert, Fray Marcos must have encountered another inhabited valley through which he traveled for three days, only to then cross a second desert which extended as far as Cíbola and which required fifteen days' travel.[37]

Following the Río Santa Cruz would bring him near Tucson; a little farther on the stream disappears into the sand. The rillito is dry except during heavy rains, and the storm season does not begin in Tucson until around the end of the month of June. The "quipatas," or days of gentle rain, which also cause the mountain streams to run, are unknown after the spring equinox. To find water it would be necessary either to plunge into the dry and sandy desert to the northwest, reaching Casa Grande or Riverside on the banks of the Gila, or to enter the Cañada del Oro and, from the old Fort Grant, attempt to cross the horrible mountains that border the Gila as far as San Carlos, or, lastly, to turn northeastward, crossing the Cebadilla, and descend into the valley of the Río San Pedro. The first of these routes seems to me to make such a considerable detour that it is out of the question,[38] and the other two finally lead to the same destination, that is, they come out at the Gila somewhere between San José del Pueblo Viejo and San Carlos.[39] If he followed the Santa Cruz, Fray Marcos must have traveled for a while among the Pimas of Sonora, and then continued on among the Pimas of Arizona.

If, however, the priest followed the Sonora valley, he arrived quite naturally at the upper course of the Río San Pedro and among the villages of the Sobaypuris, an off-shoot of the Pimas whom the Apaches forced to take refuge at San Javier del Bac around the end of the last century.[40] The dwellings of the latter began near the present settlement of Charleston, fifty kilometers north of the Mexican frontier[41] and the ruins of the villages are scattered northward throughout the valley, over a distance of at least a hundred kilometers. Therefore, I believe, until better information is available, that it was by way of the San Pedro that he reached Arizona and that he approached the Río Gila.

---

*Bandelier has these rivers inverted. The Santa Cruz flows *west* of the San Pedro.

Bandelier's Notes

[In Bandelier's notes to this chapter, *Relation* when not otherwise designated is that of Fray Marcos de Niza; Herrera's work in every case is *Historia general....*]

1. Fray Gregorio García, *Origen de los Indios,* lib. III, cap. XX, p. 189.

2. Castañeda, *Voyage de Cibola,* parte I, cap. I, p. 2; *Primera Relación anónima de la Jornada de Nuño de Guzmán,* vol. II, *Col. de documentos* by García Icazbalceta, p. 291: "And his intention was to follow that [the route] of the seven cities of which he had heard when he first left Mexico...."; *Segunda Relación anónima de la Jornada de Nuño de Guzmán, id.,* p. 303: "The object of our quest when we left to explore this river was the seven cities, because the governor, Nuño de Guzmán, had heard of them." On this subject I will take the liberty of also citing one of my own works, published in the first volume of the *Papers of the Archaeological Institute of America* and entitled *Historical Introduction to Studies among the Sedentary Indians of New Mexico,* p. 5 ...; and finally, *Cíbola (N. Yorker Staats-Zeitung),* May 1885.

3. *Segunda Relación anónima,* p. 303.

4. Matias de la Mota Padilla, *Historia de la Nueva Galicia,* cap. XXI, p. 109.

5. *Ibid.,* p. 110.

6. Fray Juan Domingo Arricivita, *Crónica seráfica y apostólica del Colegio de Propaganda fide de la Santa Cruz de Querétaro en la Nueva España,* 1792, Prólogo:

> In the year 1538, in January, Fathers Fr. Juan de la Asunción and Fr. Pedro Nadal left Mexico City, by order of the Lord Viceroy, and traveling about seven hundred leagues to the northwest, reached a very large river which they could not cross, and Father Nadal, who was well versed in mathematics, measured the elevation of the Pole as 35 degrees.

Fray Gerónimo de Mendieta, *Hist. ecclesiastica Indiana,* lib. IV, cap. XI, p. 398: "The same year of '38 he [Antonio de Ciudad Rodrigo] sent two other priests

[81]

by land and along the same coast of the Southern Sea, turning northward through Jalisco and Nueva Galicia. . . ." The details do not always agree, but they seem to relate to the same central fact.

7. Fray Antonio de Ciudad-Rodrigo, *Attestation* (in *Voyage de Cibola*, Appendix, p. 254).

8. He had already written: *"Conquista de la provincia del Quito: ritos y ceremonias de los Indios"; "Las dos Lineas de los Incas y de los Seyris en las provincias del Peru y del Quito"; "Cartas informativas de lo obrado en las provincias del Peru y del Cuzco."* See Juan de Velasco, *Histoire du royaume de Quito*, Ternaux-Compans translations, vol. XVIII and XIX, Paris, 1842. Preface, parte VIII.

9. Fray Marcos de Niza, *Accusé de réception*. (*Voyage de Cibola*, Appendix, p. 253).

10. Antonio de Mendoza, *Instruction donnée. . . . au frère Marcos de Niza* (*Voyage de Cibola*, Appendix I, p. 249). Herrera, *Hist. general*, dec. VI, lib. VII, cap. VII, pp. 155 and 156.

11. Fr. Marcos de Niza, *Relation* (*Voyage de Cíbola*, Appendix II, p. 256); Herrera, *Hist. general*, dec. VI, lib. VII, p. 156.

12. *Relation*, p. 257; Herrera, *Ibid.*, p. 156.

13. *Relation*, p. 258.

14. Orozco y Berra, *Geografía*, p. 335. According to Ribas, *Hist. de los Triumphos*, lib. II, cap. XXVII, p. 101, they were the Ahomes, also possibly the Teguecos.

15. *Relation*, p. 259; Herrera, dec. VI, p. 156.

16. Ribas, *Hist. de los Triumphos*, etc., lib. IV, cap. I, p. 236; lib. V, cap. I, p. 284; but especially lib. I, cap. III, p. 10.

17. *Relation*, p. 260; Herrera, dec. VI, p. 256.

18. P. Joseph Stocklein, *Der neue Weltbott*, vol. I, 1728. The map is also in the *Lettres édifiantes et curieuses*. Compare also the diary of Matio-Mange in the fourth series of the *Documentos para la Historia de Méjico*, 1856, vol. I, p. 327, and in the same collection the account of P. Jacob Sedelmair, S. J., *Relación que hizo. . . . misionero de Tubutama*, vol. II, pp. 846–859.

19. *Relation*, p. 260. Confirmed by Herrera.

20. This mission dates from 1629. Orozco y Berra, *Geografía*, etc., p. 344.

21. *Relation*, p. 260.

22. *Ibid.*, p. 261. Herrera gives fewer details (*Hist. general*, dec. VI, p. 157).

23. The Seris lived on the coasts and spread eastward almost as far as central Sonora; to the south, as represented by the Guaymas (one of their branch groups), they bordered on the territory of the Yaquis. Ribas, *Hist. de los Triumphos*, lib. VI, cap. I, p. 358: "it was exceedingly wild, without villages, houses or fields. They have no rivers or arroyos and drink from various ponds and puddles of water."

24. At the present time the Gila Pimas decorate their villages with strange and striking art work. The Lower Pimas live to the east of Mátape.

25. Castañeda, *Voyage de Cíbola*, parte I, cap. III, p. 11.

26. *Relation*, p. 261.

27. *Ibid.*, p. 263; Herrera (dec. VI, p. 263) says Tonteac.

28. It was because of the Mexican customs that these regular caravans were discontinued.

29. Castañeda, *Voyage de Cibola*, parte I, cap. XII, p. 72; cap. XIII, p. 77.

30. Castañeda, *Voyage de Cíbola,* p. 55; Jaramillo, *Relation,* p. 369: "This country is cold."

31. Fr. Marcos de Niza, *Relation,* pp. 264, 266, 267; Herrera (dec. VI, p. 157), is more brief, but confirms it nevertheless. This is after all quite natural, for he apparently copied Fray Marcos' account, which is at present in the Spanish archives.

32. Regarding this neutral ground, I give as a reference my work: *On the art of war and mode of warfare of the ancient Mexicans* (*19ᵗʰ Annual Report of the Peabody Museum of American Archaeology and Ethnology,* Cambridge, Mass.).

33. Mututicachi, or Motuticatzi is four *leguas* (18 kilometers) north of Bacuachi. The Sonora river sinks into the sand near there, to emerge only near the latter village. The Indian village of Mututicachi had to be abandoned because of the Apaches (*Rudo Ensayo,* cap. I, p. 13; cap. VIII, p. 192), in about 1742. North of there, the Río Sonora, in those days a small stream during the months of the year when Fray Marcos had chosen to travel, emerges from a very narrow and long *cajon,* which might well have been uninhabited in 1538.

34. *Relation,* p. 267. This remark of Friar Marcos, which I shall explain later, is based on a very true fact. Herrera (dec. VI, p. 157), is more brief, and he also says (*id.*): "and they make it of the skin of some small animals, which were the size of the Castilian greyhounds that Estevan was leading along with him."

35. *Ibid.,* p. 269. Herrera (*id.*), says: "which turns west at thirty-six degrees." It is certain that the priest was not able to get to the actual coast and return in such a short time, but he may have made a side trip in that direction and gathered information.

36. Further to the east there would also be the route by way of Fronteras (the former Corodéuachi), passing then between the Sierra Chiricahui to the east and the Sierra de las Mulas, the Sierra Peñascosa and the Sierra del Dragón, which rise above the San Simon valley. It is possible that he may have taken this route, but I believe rather that he followed the Río San Pedro downstream.

37. *Relation,* p. 272.

38. Besides, he would not have failed to notice the Pima Indian villages that were located quite nearby.

39. This part of the Gila had very few inhabitants. Some Apache "rancherías" were scattered along the river, as well as in the mountains to the north, but the inhabitants did not show themselves.

40. *Rudo Ensayo,* p. 106. The Sobaypuris abandoned their villages in 1762. Arricivita, *Crónica seráfica,* etc., lib. III, cap. XV, p. 410.

41. The ruins begin near Charleston, not only houses of rough stone and earth, but also the Sobaypuris' huts of branches and earth.

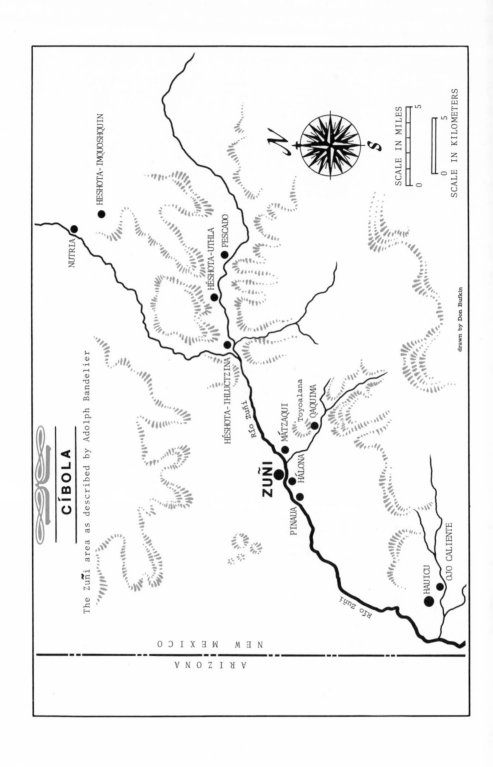

CÍBOLA

The Zuñi area as described by Adolph Bandelier

ARIZONA | NEW MEXICO

HESHOTA-IMQUOSHQUIN

NUTRIA

HÉSHOTA-UTHLA
PESCADO

HÉSHOTA-IHLIJCTZINA

Río Zuñi

MÁTZAQUI
Toyoalana
QAQUIMA

ZUÑI
HÁLONA

PINAUA

Río Zuñi

HAUICU
OJO CALIENTE

SCALE IN MILES
5
0

SCALE IN KILOMETERS
5
0

drawn by Don Bufkin

Cíbola

It is surprising that up to this point Fray Marcos mentions no river, but we must not forget that all the watercourses between the Yaqui and the Gila, even the Río Sonora, are only trickles until the summer rains swell them. After entering the large desert on May 9/21,[1] he spent the first night near a river. This river may have been the Gila. It is noteworthy here that this river is fairly wide and deep between San Carlos and the so-called Pueblo Viejo, but that nevertheless, if there is not an unusual freshet, it can be forded in several places. From the San Pedro, where the villages of the Sobaypuris come to an end, it can be reached in three days, and in eight or ten days more Zuñi is easily accessible on foot. Now, the only permanent villages built of stone, that were inhabited by natives north of the confluence of the San Pedro and the Gila in the sixteenth century and since, are the Zuñi pueblos and those of the Moquis.* So it is natural to investigate which of these groups might be Cíbola.

I will begin with the Moquis. Between 1540 and 1599, this group [of settlements] included five or seven villages.[2] However, it cannot be considered here because it is too far away. Also, in order to get there it was still necessary to pass close to Zuñi and the Indians who guided Friar Marcos would not have failed to

---

*The Moquis are the Hopi Indians of today.

point out to him the proximity of this tribe. There are other reasons that prove that Moqui cannot be Cíbola, reasons that I will mention later.

So, there remains Zuñi, and to determine whether that is the place to look for Cíbola, we must again take up the thread of the route at the entrance to the large desert which Fray Marcos still had to cross. This desert extended as far as Cíbola.

Before entering it, the friar received some fresh information about the seven cities. It is true that this information further confirmed that already received, but new details were added. Among other things, the Indians stated that the largest of the seven cities was called Ahacus. He had already heard of "Acus," but he makes a distinction between the two: "There exists also, according to this Indian's account, another very vast kingdom called Acus, for there is Ahacus and Acus. Ahacus, with the aspirate, is one of the seven cities, and the capital; Acus, without the aspirate, is a kingdom."[3] These data originated with an Indian, *native of Cíbola,* who lived in the valley which I believe to have been that of the Río San Pedro.

Estevanico, though he had gone ahead against the missionary's instructions, did not, for all that, forget certain considerations due the priest. Not only did he regularly send him news, but, in the uninhabited areas, he left behind him night shelters, one day's travel apart, so that the Father's journey, accompanied as he also was by many Indians who carried his supplies or procured them for him en route, was made with reasonable ease.[4] Thus he traveled for twelve consecutive days, "always well provided with food, deer, hare, partridges."[5]

At the end of the twelfth day, he was met by an Indian, the son of one of the chiefs who accompanied him, and who had followed the Negro Estevan.

> His face was all distraught and his body was covered with sweat; his whole appearance bore witness to much sorrow. He related to me what follows: One day, before arriving at Cíbola, Estevan, as was his custom, sent his gourd by messengers to announce his arrival. To this gourd was attached a string of bells, and two feathers, one white and the other red. When the messengers arrived before the chief who represents the ruler in this city, they

gave him the gourd. This man took it, and seeing the bells, flew into a rage, threw it onto the ground and told the messengers to leave; he said that he knew these strangers and that they should be advised not to enter the city or he would kill them all. The messengers retraced their steps and told Estevan how they had been received. He answered that it didn't matter, that those who expressed displeasure at his arrival always received him better than the others. So he continued his journey until he reached Cíbola. As he entered he encountered Indians who blocked his way; they conducted him to a large building outside the city, and immediately took from him everything he carried, exchange items, turquoises and many other gifts that he had received during his travels. He spent the night in this house without receiving anything to eat or drink. The next day, since this Indian was thirsty, he left the house to go drink at a river that flowed nearby. Soon afterwards he saw Estevan fleeing, pursued by the inhabitants of the city, who were killing the natives of his following. As soon as the Indian realized this, he followed the course of the river and managed to hide; then he turned back onto the road to the desert.[6]

These bad tidings were confirmed soon afterward. Having persuaded his people to continue on the road to Cíbola, they met, one day's travel from that spot, "two other Indians whom Estevan had taken along; they arrived covered with blood and wounds." Their accounts were only too explicit. Not only the Negro, but also almost all of his escort, had been massacred. All direct communication with Cíbola became impossible, even for the Indians, who stated "that they would no longer dare to go to Cíbola as they had been accustomed to do." To the priest's entreaties that they calm down and stop the emotional lamentations to which they had abandoned themselves, they answered: "How can we be quiet ... knowing that more than three hundred of our fathers, our sons and our brothers who went with Estevan have been killed?" They were not satisfied with refusing any further obedience to the missionary, but one of these Indians whom he had brought from Mexico City warned him that they had decided to kill him also to atone for the massacre of their relatives and their friends.[7]

This decision was not at all surprising, and conformed absolutely with the habits and customs, the ideas and principles of the natives in general. Therefore, Fray Marcos prepared himself for death; he distributed the contents of all his bundles, all the gifts intended for the inhabitants of Cíbola, among those from whose hands he expected the mortal blow. But, most of all, he wanted to see for himself the country he had so ardently longed to reach and for which he had so laboriously searched; his entreaties finally touched the hearts of his companions, the calm and resignation with which he accepted death impressed them, and a few of them finally decided to accompany him on a secret reconnaissance which was to be conducted into the vicinity of the village where Estevanico had perished.

It was around June 5 (of the year 1539)[8] that he arrived within sight of this city.

> It is built, says he, in a plain on the slope of a round height; it looks very pretty; it is the largest that I have seen in these parts. Having climbed onto a rise from whence I could observe it, I saw that the houses were built as the Indians had told me: all of stone, with several floors, and surmounted by terraces. This city is more extensive than that of Mexico. . . . Having told the chiefs who accompanied me that I found this city very beautiful, they assured me that it was the smallest of the seven cities. . . .

Finally, after having closely observed the area, he raised "a large pile of stones" on this spot, and placed a small cross on top; he then took possession of the country and retraced his steps "with much more fear than food. . . ."[9]

There is no doubt that Fray Marcos had carried out the viceroy's orders to perfection. Though exhibiting heroic courage when everyone abandoned him, he had nevertheless fulfilled the purpose of his mission without exposing either his person or his life. He has even been reproached for this caution, which has been interpreted as cowardice, when he was only doing his duty. This duty consisted in obtaining information and *bringing it to Mexico*. At the risk of his life he had gone to confirm for himself the existence of Cíbola, he had even for a moment considered entering it, "for I knew that I was only risking my life." If he did not make the attempt, the following words explain and at the same time justify his not doing so: "Finally, considering the danger, I feared that if I were killed, the knowledge of the country would be lost."[10]

He retraced his steps. The natives who had remained his friends returned in all haste to Iopax.*

> I joined them after two days' journey; I again crossed the desert with them; but I was not as well received as the first time, because the men and women were all in tears over their relatives who had been killed at Cíbola. This frightened me, and I left the inhabitants of this valley immediately. The first day I made ten leagues, then eight, then ten, without stopping, until I had crossed the second desert.

In spite of his fear, he sought and observed from afar the inhabited plain, supposedly rich in gold, of which he had heard previously along the Río Mayo,[11] and finally returned to Culiacán. Not finding Governor Coronado there, he went to Compostela to join him.[12] On September 2/14, 1539, he appeared in the capital of Mexico City, before the chief notary of the Royal Audiencia and Government of New Spain, to present to him the *Relación* that has formed the basis for this research.[13]

In any case, this report is not the only one that he wrote, for he mentions another in which he records also the names of the villages.[14] The fact that he composed two accounts explains why the one that we know of to date still leaves something to be desired as far as precise details are concerned.

To again take up the thread of the investigation on the location of Cíbola, I must go back to the point where Fray Marcos, leaving the villages of the *last* valley, entered the desert separating him from his destination. Assuming that these villages were those of the Sobaypuris, and consequently, located in the San

---

*This seems to be a misprint for "Topax." Nowhere else in his writings does Bandelier mention this name except on a map of the routes of Cabeza de Vaca and Fray Marcos de Niza which accompanies his *Histoire de la Colonisation et des Missions de Sonora, Chihuahua, Nouveau-Mexique et Arizona jusqu'à l'année 1700.* This manuscript is in the Vatican Library (still unpublished) and is being prepared for publication in English by the editor of the present article. In the portfolio of illustrations that accompanies Father Ernest J. Burrus' *Catalogue of the Bandelier Collection in the Vatican Library* (1969b), this map appears. On it, the name "Topax" is written, vertically, along the course of the San Pedro River in southern Arizona, near the Mexican border. It is not referred to anywhere in the text. It would seem to be the name of a village, but a check of Bandelier's possible sources has as yet revealed no mention of such a place, nor does Fray Marcos refer to it in his *Relación*.

Pedro valley, fifteen long days' journey would take the friar *farther* than Zuñi. On horseback I have made the trip from Zuñi to the Gila near San Carlos in eight days (without counting the stops). The Sobaypuris were, it is true, some distance south of that river, but I should also mention that I was usually going at a walk, and that, by hurrying, the journey can be made to San Carlos in six days easily. The average daily distance that I covered was twenty-six miles (44 kilometers). Fray Marcos, going on foot and guided by Indians, traveled in a straighter line, but more slowly, for the Indians showed him much consideration on the way up. On the return he made forced marches of eight or ten *leguas*[15] (the "legua" must not be confused with the French league), so he had previously done less.* A day's march of six *leguas* (or of about 27 kilometers) was a good average. Reducing the total distance that I covered, that is, three hundred and fifty-two kilometers, there still remains enough for a dozen days.† For, accompanied as he was by Indians carrying burdens, five *leguas* or twenty-two kilometers still constituted a fairly good day's march. Then too, it is not possible to go north from the Gila, and it is *necessary* to make detours, even for an Indian. The time spent by the friar in reaching Cíbola would then correspond approximately to the distance that separates the Río San Pedro from Zuñi.[16] To reach the Moquis, three to five days more would be required.

Cíbola was in a plain on the slope of a round height.[17] All the Moqui pueblos were and still are built on the tops of high, dry mesas, separated by small valleys.[18] Zuñi is different. The little river that bears this name rises east of the present pueblo and

---

*Although various historians have evaluated the Spanish league at everything from a little over 2 miles to as much as 4 miles, the generally accepted equivalent seems to be about 2.6 miles. The French league was slightly different, as Bandelier points out, probably about 2.8 miles.

†Bandelier's calculations here appear rather confused, since he does not stay with the same system of measurement throughout. However, what he seems to be trying to say is that Fray Marcos probably took a more direct, hence shorter route than he did, since the Franciscan was traveling on foot. Even with the detours required, men could walk where a horse might have difficulty. But Bandelier assumes that, even if Fray Marcos covered less actual distance than he did to reach the same destination, it would still take the friar at least twelve days, since his progress was slower.

northeast of the village called Pescado, about eighty-five kilometers from the Arizona border, in New Mexico. Its average direction is southwest, and it enters the area bordered by the Merced (or the deeded land of the Zuñi Indians), near Pescado. The latter is an ancient pueblo of this tribe, still partially occupied today, and which they call Héshota Izina. From there, the little river flows through a narrow and desolate valley for about twenty-five kilometers, passing near the ruined villages of Héshota-Uthla and Héshota-Ihluctzina; then, almost at the foot of an isolated and formidable rock called Zuñi Mesa, it enters a sandy plain twenty-five kilometers long by fifteen to twenty wide from north to south. This plain is the Zuñi plain, and is surrounded by moderate heights covered with fir and juniper. This monotonous fringe area is dominated by three enormous rocks with steep cliffs, which tower over it and loom above it like so many giants. Two of these colossi rise up north of the plain, the third and most famous closes it in abruptly on the eastern side. This monster is ten kilometers long and stands one thousand twenty-six English feet in height above the plain, from which its walls rise almost everywhere in vertical sections. The few trails that lead to the summit are barely passable, just managing to cling to the rock, and the climber hovers, so to speak, over ever deepening chasms. The summit is a plateau partially covered with juniper and a few pines; there is good arable land and natural ponds with water that lasts all year if care is taken to clean them and to increase their content by piling snow up in them in winter. The Zuñis call this table-like mountain To-yo-a-la-na, or Thunder Mountain; they took refuge there after 1680, and on the top built six villages the ruins of which have been erroneously called Old Zuñi by the Anglo-Americans.[19] It was only after 1705 that they were induced to come down into the plain where they settled in the present pueblo.[20]

I shall always remember the first impression that the view of these colossi of reddish sandstone made on me. I saw them as I emerged from a vast thicket of juniper in which I had been wandering for six hours on foot, alone and unarmed. I had eaten nothing for twenty hours and for twelve hours I had been without water. I was looking for Zuñi. It was a calm day, but the sky was overcast and snow threatened. Emerging from the brush, I saw the plateaus stretching before me in all directions like a dark table cloth under a gray sky. Only to the southeast were there enormous pillars of rock rising in the distance, like motionless elephants. The sun ripped the clouds apart for a moment; its rays, striking the red cliffs, transformed the pillars temporarily into columns of fire. Then the sky again became overcast and a storm began to build. I was still fifteen kilometers away from the plain and I entered it at the moment when the first sandy dust devils began to cross it, moaning as they went, and when lightning struck the nearest colossus. The storm was of short duration; then night fell, a black night without stars, cold and calm. The most complete shadows enveloped me, I walked blindly and stumbling. Finally the sky became a little lighter, the moon was rising behind the clouds, stars began to pierce through at the zenith. Around eight o'clock in the evening I distinguished the contours of a hill over which floated a mist. It was my first sight of the pueblo of Zuñi where I had the pleasure of spending some enjoyable days with my friend Cushing.

There are several ruins of Zuñi villages in the plain. Three of them were inhabited until 1680. These were Ha-lo-na, on the ruins of which stands today's Zuñi, Qa-quima, in a niche formed by the south walls of the great Thunder Mesa, and Mâ-tza-qui, northwest of that mesa, near its base.[21] There is also Pî-na-ua, five kilometers southwest of the present village, and two other ruins toward the northern end of the plain. In 1580, Francisco Sánchez Chamuscado visited Zuñi and mentioned six villages;[22] in 1583, Espejo found six,[23] and the same number is mentioned by Oñate in 1598.[24] However, it is not certain that all the pueblos in the plain were inhabited in the sixteenth century. Fifteen miles (25 kilometers) southwest of Zuñi, near the hot springs *(Aguas calientes)*,* there stood until 1679 the large village of Ha-ui-cu,† which had to be abandoned in 1679 because of the incursions of the Apaches,[25] and twenty-five miles (41 kilometers) to the northeast, in the beautiful Nutria valley, there are, besides the little pueblo of Nutria or To-ya, which the Zuñis still

*Now known as Ojo Caliente.
†Bandelier consistently uses this spelling, though more recent scholars seem to prefer "Hawikuh."

occupy today during the summer, the vast ruins of Hésho-ta Im-quosh-quin. Thus there are, in the Zuñi plain alone, six villages of which at least three were undoubtedly occupied in the sixteenth century. From the heights that dominate the plain to the south all six villages can be encompassed in a single glance. It was from the south that Fray Marcos de Niza cautiously approached the "plain" of Cíbola.

I cannot mention Zuñi without including in that mention an affectionate testimonial of esteem and gratitude for the excellent friend to whom I owe my most precious information concerning this tribe, its customs, and the traditions of its past. Mr. *Frank Hamilton Cushing* spent four years among the tribe for purely *scientific* purposes. To his research we owe the first systematic and comprehensive information about their religious organization, their rituals, their beliefs. He has opened up to us the vast field of Indian mythology, which, until now, had been a confused labyrinth filled with mystery. With unusual generosity he communicated to me the precious results of his research, and if I take advantage of it, it is to recognize in him the source of all the facts related to the Zuñi tribe, other than travel impressions or extracts from more or less ancient writers.

It is to Mr. Cushing that we owe the knowledge of the real name of the country and of the tribe of Zuñi. This name is Shi-ua-na, and they call themselves A Shi-ui.[26] The name Zuñi appears for the first time in Spanish documents of 1598, and they heard it along the Río Grande, at San Juan and at Santo Domingo, in other words among the Jehuas [Tehuas] and the Queris [Queres].[27] From the official documents of that period, it passed into general usage, and since the Castilian language became the means of oral communication between the various pueblos,[28] this name was generally adopted. Shi-ua-na does not lack a certain distant analogy to Cíbola, especially if we allow ourselves to assume that Fray Marcos, being from Nice, wrote *Ci*, but perhaps still pronounced it *Chi!** This is possible, but

---

*Bandelier seems to assume here that Fray Marcos' native language was Italian, though in his *Contributions to the History of the Southwestern United States* (1890*a*), published four years after this article, he definitely quotes evidence that Fray Marcos was French.

hardly probable.[29] Nevertheless, there are, in New Mexico as in Arizona, Indian names just as distorted as is Cíbola by comparison with Shi-ua-na. I shall mention here: *Pa-yo-go-no*, changed to *Pecos*, *Hae-mish* to *Jemez*, *Or-li-son* to *Arizona*, *Styucson* to *Tucson*.[30]

Without dwelling on an analogy of sounds, which may be merely a coincidence, I will pass on to the event that represented the critical moment in Friar Marcos' undertaking: the arrival of the Negro at Cíbola and his death. Such an event leaves a deep impression in the memory of Indian tribes; it becomes the subject of a very definite tradition. This tradition is communicated orally from generation to generation and it is only after many centuries, when it has ceased to be of any immediate importance, that it takes refuge within the more restricted circle of educated men. The tradition then becomes a religious myth, and as such remains the property of the esoteric groups.

In spite of all the research carried on among the tribes of the Southwest, it had been impossible to find any trace of the passage of the Negro or of Fray Marcos. There were recollections of the Coronado expedition which was undertaken the following year, but of the journey of the two others there remained no trace in the natives' memory. After several years of residence in Zuñi, however, Mr. Cushing, through his initiation into the secret and ritual orders, picked up the two following traditions.

According to the first, a man accompanied by *two dogs* was said to have arrived in Zuñi long before the arrival of the first Spaniards; this man was called Nu-é; he seemed famished and seized all the food that he could find, without asking permission. This so annoyed the natives that the chiefs, during the night, gave him a big kick that made him disappear into the southern regions.

The second tradition is more clearly outlined. According to it, there arrived one day in the Zuñi plain a *black Mexican*. This man entered the pueblo of *Qa-quima*, where he very quickly rendered himself so hateful by his licentious conduct that they were obliged to restrain him. He was not willing to submit. So they killed him! Shortly afterward, many *Mexicans* arrived in the area with horses and weapons. They made war upon the people of Zuñi and since that time they have remained masters of the country.* (The Zuñi Indian only knows the Spaniards as Spaniards of *Mexico;* he consequently calls them Mexicans without making any distinction between them and those of Europe.)

These traditions have the value of being authentic inasmuch as they are purely Indian and peculiar to Zuñi, and are ancient and not created or modified by foreign intrusions. Therefore, it is history, and this history tells us that a *Negro* was *killed at Qa-quima.* The two traditions relate to the same facts, but, since the Zuñi of today (called Halona by its inhabitants) is peopled by the descendants of the six or seven ancient pueblos, and each pueblo preserved (and still preserves) its local traditions, that of Qaquima is more definite, agrees more with the events than does the first, which, originating in places where the Negro had never even been seen, merely reflects certain aspects of the story and even those only vaguely.

Mr. Cushing, as well as myself, struck as we were by the resemblance of the word Nu-é to Nuñez, thought that this first story had reference to Alvar Núñez Cabeza de Vaca. But, since the latter was never in New Mexico, it is clear that it is not of him that the Indian tradition speaks, but of the Negro, and the dogs that accompanied him were the two greyhounds mentioned in Father Marcos' account.[31]

Thus there are pretty certain indications here that it is *in the Zuñi plain that Cíbola should be sought,* and that the village where Estevanico was killed is the now ruined pueblo of Qaquima.

This pueblo is located on a mound of rubble, set, so to speak, in a niche at the foot of the immense vertical cliffs that constitute the southern face of the huge Zuñi mesa.[32] The French translation of Fray Marcos' account says that Cíbola was *on the slope of a hill,* round in shape [sur les flancs d'une colline de forme ronde], but the original Spanish uses the term *cerro de forma*

---

*This story is given in more detail by Cushing in his "The Discovery of Zuñi, or the Ancient Provinces of Cíbola and the Seven Lost Cities," a lecture which he gave before the Geographic Society of Boston in 1885. It is quoted in part in Green 1979. The original is at the Southwest Museum, Los Angeles, in the Hodge–Cushing Collection.

rodonda [sic].*[33] Now, a cerro, in an already mountainous country, is not a hill, but in fact an isolated mountain such as the great
mesa appears to be from a distance. Redondo was used (and is
still used today in New Mexico) to designate anything that has
more than three sides; thus, in the pueblos, the open plazas,
which are always square, are referred to as *como redondas.*

There were, in the old days, on the heights that dominate the
plain to the south (thus opposite Qaquima) the remains of a
wooden cross! Might they have been the remains of the cross
that Fray Marcos planted overlooking the plain of Cíbola? In the
dry climate of New Mexico, beams, even splinters (constituting
part of the ancient roofs of ruined pueblos) are still enduring
today, though without the protection of the layer of earth that
covered them originally. And these pueblos were abandoned
long before the sixteenth century.

In addition to the already rather conclusive evidence that I
have just mentioned, there are other things that identify Zuñi
with Cíbola beyond any doubt. I shall begin with the least
important.

Besides Cíbola, Fray Marcos speaks of a so-called kingdom named Acus. This is the pueblo of Acoma situated to the
east of Zuñi at a distance of about one hundred and fifty kilometers, and which the Zuñis call either Ha-cu-quin, or simply
Ha-cu.[34]

He makes the distinction, as I have mentioned, between Acus
and Ahacus, saying that the latter name is that of one of the
seven cities. Ahacus is indeed Ha-ui-cu, or the ancient peublo
near the Aguas Calientes of Zuñi.

Marata is another name of a locality that he mentions.

> He told me that to the southeast lies a kingdom called Marata,
> that there are large settlements there; that all have stone houses
> several stories high; that they are still fighting with the ruler of
> the seven cities. According to him, this war has greatly weakened
> the strength of the kingdom of Marata; but nevertheless it is still
> powerful and continues to defend itself.

---

*The correct quotation is: "a la falda de un cerro redondo." (See Fray Marcos
de Niza, *Relación*, in Pacheco *et al.* 1864–84, Vol. II, 1st Series, p. 347.)

There is a very interesting fact here. The man who told these things to Friar Marcos was a native of Cíbola and very old. He had left that country to take refuge among the Sobaypuris. He therefore was telling him about events that were not recent, but which nevertheless had taken place while this Indian was still living in Cíbola. Now, Marata is Ma-tyâta, as Mr. Cushing has very well recognized, and Ma-tyâta is the name given by the Indians of Zuñi to the group of ruined pueblos in the vicinity of the salt lake called El Carrizo, located nearly two days' journey south of Zuñi. The fact that these pueblos were abandoned before 1539 is brought out in the report that Melchior Díaz made the following year to the viceroy of New Spain,[35] but it seems that their destruction only took place around the beginning of the sixteenth century. The present state of these ruins does indeed indicate that the period of their abandonment must have been comparatively recent.[36]

Finally, mention is often made of the country of Totonteac. This was situated west or northwest of Zuñi–Cíbola.[37] The word is corrupted, distorted, misunderstood, and consequently misspelled. According to Mr. Cushing's findings, this is an ancient expression in the Zuñi language designating the regions to the west, and the name applies to the *Moquis*.

In conclusion, I shall cite evidence that dates from after Fray Marcos' expedition, since it is taken from the accounts of the campaign in New Mexico that Francisco Vásquez Coronado commanded in 1540–44.* The most detailed of these accounts is that of Castañeda, but Jaramillo, though much less exact, has already made a rather important observation. He says: "All the watercourses that we encountered, both creeks and rivers, as far as that of Cíbola, and I think even as much as a day or two beyond, flow toward the Southern Sea; further on they flow toward the Northern Sea."[38] All the watercourses east of Zuñi, as far as the Río Grande del Norte, do indeed flow into the latter river, and consequently into the Mexican Gulf, while the Río Zuñi itself is a confluent of the Río Colorado Chiquito [Little

---

*This is probably a misprint in the text. The Coronado expedition returned to Mexico in 1542.

Colorado], and through it, of the greater Colorado, thus empty-
ing into the Gulf of California and the Southern Sea.

Pedro Castañeda says of Cíbola: "It is a very narrow valley
between steep mountains. The province of Cíbola contains
seven villages; the largest is called Muzaque."[39] So writes the
French translator* [C'est une vallée très étroite entre des mon-
tagnes escarpées. La province de Cíbola contient sept villages; le
plus grand se nomme Muzaque.], but the original manuscript,
which I have been able to consult, clearly and definitely says
Maçaqui.[40]

Now, Maçaqui or Mâtzaqui was indeed one of the largest
Zuñi pueblos. Today it is in ruins, and these ruins are located,
as I have already mentioned, northwest of the great mesa or
Thunder Mountain, nearly at the edge of the plain. The estab-
lishment of the church of La Purificación at Halona after 1598
caused the population to gravitate almost imperceptibly toward
the latter village, so that in 1680[41] Matzaqui was reduced to a
simple hamlet (aldea). Abandoned shortly after 1680, it was
never resettled. But tradition states, and the ruins prove, that
Matzaqui was formerly the largest pueblo of all those in the
Zuñi plain.

So there is no doubt that Zuñi is Cíbola and, since Zuñi is
located in New Mexico, to Friar Marcos of Nice belongs the
honor of being the first to acquaint the civilized world of Spain
and Europe with this country and its sedentary native peoples.
The Negro, who was supposed to be his guide and companion,
disobeyed him in order to capture from him the laurels of discovery. His disobedience cost him his life, whilst the friar, by
doing his duty, not only was able to reach his proposed goal, but
succeeded also in bringing back the information that later led to
the conquest and finally the colonization of the lands that he
discovered.

Fray Marcos' accounts have been strongly criticized since
then. He has been treated as an exaggerator, even, to put it
bluntly, as a liar, an impostor. A little more than a year after his

---

*Bandelier did not have the original Spanish text at hand at the time when he
was writing this article and worked from the French translation of Ternaux-
Compans. He had, however, previously seen the original.

return to Mexico City, when he arrived at Zuñi with the advance guard of Coronado's expedition, he was forced to return to New Spain in order to escape the anger of the soldiers who claimed that he had deceived them.[42] We have no idea what he may have said verbally on the subject of Cíbola.[43] As for those of his writings that remain to us their facts are *surprisingly accurate.*

I have already demonstrated this from a geographical standpoint; there now remains the ethnographic aspect of his report. That is the one that has been the most vigorously attacked. Here we must carefully distinguish between what the missionary-explorer said he had himself seen, and what he says he heard from others.

If he speaks of thousands of "cowhides" in Sonora, it is an exaggeration or misunderstanding on his part. It is probable that he may have seen bison hides, but that he was unable to make the distinction between these and the skins of the large dark deer of these regions, never having himself seen the American buffalo.[44] As for the turquoises, the Opatas, like the Pimas, had them and wore them. They adorned themselves generally with all kinds of green and blue stones. Silicate and carbonate of copper, green apatite, were used as well as kalinite. The latter mineral is found, polished, cut and perforated, in almost all the ruins in the Southwest. It is not rare in New Mexico, where it is particularly plentiful in the rock south of the city of Santa Fé,[45] as well as in the vicinity of of Zuñi! The priest may have been mistaken about the large quantity of these stones, but it is still certain that they constituted a fairly common ornament among the natives. In Zuñi, as in all the New Mexican pueblos, there are even great numbers of them. What they told him about the turquoises set in the doors in Cíbola was absolutely true. This custom of setting small stones of this kind in the wooden frames around the openings through which they entered the rooms by means of ladders, especially in the *estufas* or meeting places, existed from ancient times, as Mr. Cushing discovered. Today it has fallen into disuse.

The small animals "the size of the two greyhounds that Estevan was leading with him" and of which, in Totonteac, a gray fabric was made similar to the cloth of the friar's habit, were none other than hares and rabbits. The Moqui Indians cut their skins into very fine strips and twist strands of them in with cords of pita or yucca fibre. Fuzzy thongs the thickness of a little finger result, and these thongs are braided or woven in such a way as to form very thick blankets, which these Indians still wear today in winter. I have even found fragments of rabbit hair fabrics at the source of the Río Gila, in rock shelters (cave-dwellings) in New Mexico. So this fact too is quite correct, and also confirms the previous conclusions that Totonteac must refer to the group of Moqui villages.

If Fray Marcos speaks of kingdoms, rulers, cities and provinces, to designate simple villages and their elected chiefs, he should not be blamed. This was the terminology, the nomenclature of the period, and it still is among many writers of today who have no thorough knowledge of the American Indian nor of his social and religious organization. As for the seven-story houses, it is unnecessary to mention that in Zuñi, as well as in Taos, some still exist today with at least five stories.

However, the complaint that, more than any other, seems to have a firm foundation, is the one that is based on the Franciscan's statement that Cíbola was larger than Mexico City; this complaint seems all the more justified in that Coronado's soldiers were already making it one year later. Nevertheless, any pueblo, with its tall multi-storied houses, appears at a distance to be much larger than it is in reality. Anyone, especially, who is unfamiliar with the inhabitants' way of life, who does not know that the lower rooms are almost never occupied, always overestimates the population of an Indian village of this type. But there is another even more decisive point. Fray Marcos was comparing Qaquima, not with the former large Mexican pueblo of Tenochtitlan[46] that had been razed and which he had never seen, but with the *new Spanish city* of Mexico that he knew. At that time this city had existed for barely eighteen years.[47] During the first years of the seventeenth century, sixty years later, Mexico City contained four thousand Spanish residents,[48] and it is, I repeat, of the young Spanish city that the friar speaks, and not of the Indian quarter of Tlatelolco, which Cervantes-Salazar describes in 1554 about fifteen years later, as consisting of "indorum acciculae [sic],* quas quia humiles sunt et humi serpunt, intra nostratia aedificia obequitantes conspicere non potuimus."†49 So, if any possible exaggeration exists, it is natural and involuntary, and the comparison is even far from being out of line.

So the bold undertaking of the friar from Nice resulted not only in the discovery of New Mexico, but also in very accurate accounts of the customs and manners of its most interesting inhabitants. These things gave rise to the expedition of Francisco Vásquez de Coronado. The latter was acquainted with what the priest had *reported in writing.* I believe that I have shown above that these reports were in keeping with the truth. So, if Coronado failed in his attempt at colonization,50 this failure cannot be attributed to the supposed errors of Friar Marcos.

---

*The original text reads "indiorum aediculae." (See Cervantes–Salazar 1953, facsimile fol. 271v.)

†"Indian dwellings, which from horseback we could not see among our buildings, because they are humble and lie low to the ground."

Bandelier's Notes

[In Bandelier's notes to this chapter, *Relation* not otherwise designated is that of Fray Marcos de Niza.]

1. *Relation*, p. 273.
2. There is no doubt that Castañeda's Tusayan is Moqui. Compare Simpson, *Coronado's march* (in *Smithsonian Report* of 1869). Tusayan consisted of seven villages. [Castañeda] *Voyage de Cibola*, p. 58; Jaramillo, *Relation*, p. 370. In 1584, Espejo visited the Moquis, and he noted five pueblos there, to which he gave the name of Mohece (*Relación del viaje*, p. 118). It is impossible to determine the reason for this difference. In 1598–99, Juan de Oñate mentions five also. See *Obediencia y Vasallaje a su Magestad por los Indios de la Provincia de Mohoqui* in *Documentos Inéditos*, vol. XV, p. 137; *Obediencia y Vassallaje por los Indios de Aguatobi. Ibidem.*
3. *Relation*, p. 271.
4. *Relation*, pp. 267, 274. These huts were sometimes of earth, sometimes of tree branches. If he had traveled through the country west of Tucson he would have been glad not to use them, because of the heat and the insects!
5. *Ibid.*, p. 274.
6. *Relation*, pp. 274–278; Herrera, *Hist. general*, dec. VI, lib. VII, cap. VIII, pp. 157–159.
7. *Relation*, p. 277; Herrera, p. 159.
8. Having entered the desert on May 9/12, the priest traveled through it until May 21, or June 2, before encountering the Indian who brought him the news of the Negro's death (p. 276). By adding the three days to make up the fifteen that he estimated were necessary, we come to June 5, or to some day between the 5th and the 10th of the month. Herrera copies the Franciscan's account almost word for word.
9. *Relation*, p. 280. Herrera is a little less explicit.
10. *Relation*, p. 280. Herrera, *Hist. general*, dec. VI, p. 159: "and Fr. Marcos states that he was tempted to enter the city; but that he considered

that, if he died, no report could be made about this land which seemed to him the best of any that had been discovered."

11. *Relation,* p. 257, 281; Herrera, p. 159.

12. *Relation,* p. 282.

13. Juan Baiza de Herrera, *Attestation,* p. 283.

14. *Relation,* p. 262.

15. *Relation,* p. 280 to 281; Herrera, p. 159.

16. From Zuñi to Fort Apache, it is 120 miles by the present route which is the easiest; from Fort Apache to the Río Gila it is 68, in all about 300 kilometers. From the Río Gila to the San Pedro, by way of Fort Grant (the new garrison) 2 or 3 days' travel is required.

17. *Relation,* p. 279; Herrera, p. 159: "which is situated in a plain, on the slope of a round height."

18. *Contributions to North American Ethnology* (vol. IV, L. H. Morgan, Houses and House-Life of the American Aborigines, p. 141): "They are seven in number, situated upon mesa elevations within an extent of ten miles, difficult of access, and constructed of stone." [Quoted in English.]

19. It is such a well-known fact that, in support, I cite only Diego de Vargas. Ms., Santa Fe Archives, 1694: "On this extensive mesa more than two leagues in area, lived the natives of the above-mentioned Zuñi nation, [who came] from its five pueblos which had been depopulated by their enemies the Apaches."

20. *Gobierno de D. Francisco Cubero y Valdés* (vol. II, *Documentos para la Historia de México,* 3rd Series, vol. I, p. 190).

21. Fray Agustín de Vetancurt, *Crónica de la Provincia del Santo Evangelio de México,* 1870 edition, pp. 320 to 321.

22. *Testimonio dado en México sobre el descubrimiento de doscientos leguas adelante,* pp. 85–92. He calls it Cami.

23. Antonio de Espejo, *Relación,* p. 177. He calls Zuñi "Amé, Ami."

24. *Obediencia y vasallaje por los Indios de la Provincia de Zuñi* (*Doc. Inéd.,* vol. XV).

25. Fray Silvestre Vélez de Escalante, *Carta.* (*Doc. para la Historia de México,* 3rd Series, vol. I, p. 116).

26. Cushing, *Zuñi Fetishes,* pp. 9, etc.

27. *Obediencia y Vasallaje a Su Magestad de San Juan Baptista* (*Doc. Inéd.,* vol. XV, p. 114, etc.); *Obediencia, etc., de Santo Domingo.* (*Ibid.,* pp. 116–118).

28. At the present time, the different linguistic groups communicate in Spanish.

29. Ramusio (*Terzio Volume del Navigatione et Viaggi,* 556, pp. 357–363) writes Cenola.

30. There are still many others. Thus: Ta-ui to Taos, Potzua-ge to Pojuague, Te-tzo-ge to Tezuque, etc.

31. *Relation,* p. 267.

32. *To-yo-a-la-na.*

33. Herrera writes *cerro redondo.*

34. Acoma is properly called Aco or Acoma.

35. Antonio de Mendoza, *Deuxième lettre à l'empereur Charles V.* (In *Cíbola,* Appendix, p. 295.)

36. Sections of wall still exist to a height of three stories.

37. Mendoza (*Deuxième lettre*, p. 296) says that Melchior Díaz confirms what Fray Marcos said about Totonteac.
38. Jaramillo, *Relation*, p. 370.
39. [Castañeda] *Voyage de Cíbola*, parte II, cap. III, p. 163.
40. The original is in the Lenox Library [now part of New York Public Library]. The title is as stated by Mr. Ternaux-Compans, and Maçaque is found twice, parte II, cap. III, fol. 107 recto.
41. Vargas, *Aulto de Remission* (ms.); Vetancurt, *Crónica* (p. 320): "with two villages called Mazaquia [and Caquima], which were 'visitas', each with its own little church. . . ." [Ed. note: Usually a priest was responsible for more than one mission in an area. The main church was located in the "cabecera" where the priest had his headquarters. The others were "visitas," churches that he visited from time to time when he made the circuit of his missions.]
42. Castañeda, *Voyage de Cíbola*, pp. 42 and 48.
43. *Ibid.*, pp. 16 and 30.
44. He speaks (p. 271) of a skin

> . . . one and a half times larger than the skin of a cow; they told me that it belonged to an animal that had only one horn on the forehead, this horn curves back toward the chest, from there it turns up again at right angles. . . . (p. 272.) The color resembles that of the goat, the hair is the length of a finger. [Quoted in French by Bandelier.]

This may well have been the only buffalo hide that he saw.
45. At the Cerrillos.
46. Tenochtitlán covered a quarter of the area of the present city of Mexico. On this subject, see my *An Archaeological Tour into Mexico*, part II, pp. 49 and 50.
47. The oldest book of the municipality of the city of Mexico begins on March 8, 1524: *Actas de Cabildo de la Ciudad de México*, prim. libr. published by the licenciate Ignacio Rayon, 1877, p. 3. According to S. Joaquín García Icazbalceta, it was around 1523 that the municipality was moved from Cuyucan to the new settlement. See *México en 1554, tres Diálogos latinos que Francisco Cervantes Salazar escribió e imprimió en México en dicho año*, p. 74, note 74. So in 1539, Mexico City had been in existence for about 16 years. According to Rodrigo de Albornoz, *Carta al Emperador*, December 15, 1525 (*Col. de Doc.*, vol. I, p. 506): "to make this city permanent, nearly one hundred and fifty Spanish houses have been built there, and many Indian ones." In 1556, Mexico City contained 1,500 Spaniards according to Thomson (Hackluyt [sic], *Voyages*, vol. III, p. 539). [Ed. note: Though Bandelier says 1556, this statement was taken from "The Voyage of Robert Tomson, marchant, into Nova Hispania in the yere 1555." See Hakluyt, 1904, vol. IX, p. 355.]
48. Herrera, *Historia general, Descripción*, vol. I, cap. IX, p. 17.
49. *Tres Diálogos latinos*, p. 136.
50. However, Castañeda reproaches him strongly, but this can only be based on the words and not on the writings of the priest. In any case, Castañeda is a very unreliable writer on this subject. Thus, he says, speaking of the return of Melchior Díaz (pp. 29–30): "Having found nothing remarkable. . . . the bad news that they brought back. . . ." [Ed. note: The complete quotation is: "It seems that at the time when General Francisco Vásquez left Culiacán with

Fray Marcos to give the above-mentioned information to the viceroy, Don Antonio de Mendoza, he had left orders for Captain Melchior Díaz and Juan de Zaldívar, with a dozen good men, to leave Culiacán to search for what Fray Marcos had seen and heard about. They started off and went as far as Chichilticale, which is the beginning of the *despoblado* or uninhabited area, 220 leagues from Culiacán. Not finding anything worthwhile, they returned, arriving at the time when the army was about to leave Chiametla. They reported to the general, but no matter how secretly it was done, the bad news soon spread." (Castañeda de Naçera 1896, part I, chap. VII).] Now Melchior Díaz confirms everything that the priest said about Cíbola. Compare his account in the *Deuxième lettre* of the viceroy, pp. 292–297. He [Casteñeda] also has the audacity to say that Fray Marcos never saw Cíbola, and the accusation of cowardice originates *mainly with him* (pp. 13 and 14). Finally, he accuses him of having given Coronado "such a grandiose description of everything that the Negro discovered, of what the Indians had told them, and of the islands filled with riches which they had been assured existed in the Southern Sea. . . ." (p. 16). Of all that, there is not a word in the Franciscan friar's account. But these slanderous remarks spread far and wide, and for three centuries and more the preferred course has been to rehash them from time to time, rather than investigate the places themselves and thus make an impartial and intelligent judgment.

Reference Material

Selected Bibliography

Albornoz, Rodríguez de
1858,1866   "Carta del Contador Rodríguez de Albornoz, al Emperador." In *Colección de documentos para la historia de México*, edited by J. García–Icazbalceta, vol. 1, pp. 484–511. Mexico City: Antigua Librería.

Alegre, Francisco Javier
1841   *Historia de la Compañía de Jesús en Nueva España*. Edited by Carlos María Bustamante. 3 vols. Mexico City: J. M. Lara.
1956   *Historia de la Compañía de Jesús en Nueva España*. Edited by Ernest J. Burrus, S.J., and Félix Zubillaga, S.J. 4 vols. Rome: Institutum Historicum S.J.

Anonymous
1858,1866   "Primera Relación Anónima de la Jornada que hizo Nuño de Guzmán a la Nueva Galicia." In *Colección de documentos para la historia de México*, edited by J. García–Icazbalceta, vol. 2, pp. 288–294. Mexico City: Antigua Librería.

Anonymous
1858,1866   "Segunda Relación Anónima de la Jornada que hizo Nuño de Guzmán a la Nueva Galicia." In *Colección de documentos para la historia de México*, edited by J. García–Icazbalceta, vol. 2, pp. 296–306. Mexico City: Antigua Librería.

Arricivita, Juan Domingo
1792   *Crónica seráfica y apostólica del Colegio de propaganda fide de la Santa Cruz de Querétaro de la Nueva España*. 2 vols. Mexico City: Felipe de Zúñiga y Ontiveras.

Arteaga y S., Armando
1932   "Fray Marcos de Niza y el descubrimiento de Nuevo México."
            Hispanic American Historical Review, vol. 12, November, pp. 481–
            489.

Baldwin, Percy M.
1926   "Fray Marcos de Niza and his Discovery of the Seven Cities
            of Cíbola." *New Mexico Historical Review*, vol. 1, April, pp. 193–
            223.

Bandelier, Adolph F.
1877   "On the Art of War and Mode of Warfare of the Ancient Mexi-
            cans." *Tenth Annual Report of the Peabody Museum of American
            Archaeology and Ethnology*, pp. 95–161. Cambridge, Mass.
1878   "On the Distribution and Tenure of Lands, and the Customs with
            Respect to Inheritance, among the Ancient Mexicans." *Eleventh
            Annual Report of the Peabody Museum of American Archaeology and
            Ethnology*, pp. 385–448. Cambridge, Mass.
1880   "On the Social Organization and Mode of Government of the
            Ancient Mexicans." *Twelfth Annual Report of the Peabody Museum
            of American Archaeology and Ethnology* [1879], pp. 557–699. Cam-
            bridge, Mass.
1881   *Historical Introduction to Studies among the Sedentary Indians of New
            Mexico and a Visit to the Aboriginal Ruins in the Valley of the Río
            Pecos*. Archaeological Institute of America, American Series, vol.
            1, nos. 1, 2. Boston: A. Williams; London: N. Trübner. Reprint.
            Millwood, N.Y.: Kraus Reprint Co., 1976.
1884   *Report of an Archaeological Tour in Mexico in 1881*. Archaeological
            Institute of America, American Series, vol. 2. Boston: Cupples,
            Upham and Co.; London: N. Trübner. Reprint. Millwood, N.Y.:
            Kraus Reprint Co., 1976.
1885   "Cíbola I," (parts 1–7), *New Yorker Staatszeitung, Sonntagsblatt*,
            May 24, 31; June 7, 14, 21, 28; July 5. "Cibola II," (parts 1–4), *ibid.*
            October 25; November 1, 8, 15.
1886a   "Alvar Nuñez Cabeza de Vaca, the First Overland Traveler of
            European Descent, and his Journey from Florida to the Pacific
            Coast, 1528–1536." *Magazine of Western History*, vol. 4, no. 3, July,
            pp. 327–336. (Misprinted on title page as vol. 5.)
1886b   "La Découverte du Nouveau Mexique par le Moine Franciscain
            Frère Marcos de Nice en 1539." *Revue d'Ethnographie*, January–
            February, pp. 31–48; March–April, pp. 117–134; May–June, pp.
            193–212.
1886c   "The Discovery of New Mexico by Fray Marcos de Nizza."
            Magazine of Western History, vol. 4, no. 5, pp. 659–670. Reprint.
            New Mexico Historical Review, vol. 4, no. 1, pp. 28–44, 1929. Also
            in *The Mesoamerican Southwest: Readings in Archaeology, Ethnohis-
            tory and Ethnology*, edited by B. C. Hedrick, J. C. Kelley and C.
            L. Riley. Carbondale, Ill.: Southern Illinois University Press, 1974.

Condensed version in *The Masterkey,* vol. 2, no. 8, April 1929, pp. 5–15.

1887   *Histoire de la colonisation et des missions de Sonora, Chihuahua, Nouveau-Mexique et Arizona jusqu'à l'année 1700.* Manuscript in the Vatican Library, Rome (Vat. Lat. 14111–14116, unpublished). 1,400 foolscap pages, 502 watercolor drawings, photographs and maps. 5 vols. and Atlas. English translation by Madeleine Turrell Rodack (unpublished). Typescript, Jesuit Historical Institute Collection, Arizona State Museum, University of Arizona, Tucson, Arizona.

1890*a*   *Contributions to the History of the Southwestern Portion of the United States: Hemenway Southwestern Archaeological Expedition.* Archaeological Institute of America, American Series, vol. 5. Cambridge: John Wilson and Son, University Press. Reprint. Millwood, N.Y.: Kraus Reprint Co., 1976.

1890*b*   *The Delight Makers.* Introduction by Charles F. Lummis. New York: Dodd, Mead and Co. Reprint. New York: Dodd Mead and Co., 1916, 1946; Fanny R. Bandelier, 1918; New York: Harcourt Brace Jovanovich, 1971.

1890–1892   *Final Report of Investigations among the Indians of the Southwestern United States, Carried on Mainly in the Years from 1880 to 1885:* Parts 1, 2. Archaeological Institute of America, American Series, vols. 3, 4. Cambridge: John Wilson and Son, University Press. Reprint. Millwood, N.Y.: Kraus Reprint Co., 1976.

1893   *The Gilded Man (El Dorado) and other Pictures of the Spanish Occupancy of America.* New York: D. Appleton and Co. Reprint. Chicago: The Rio Grande Press, 1962.

1937   See Hewett, Edgar L.

Bandelier, Fanny Ritter, trans.
1905   *The Journey of Alvar Nuñez Cabeza de Vaca and His Companions from Florida to the Pacific, 1528–1536.* Introduction by Adolph F. Bandelier. New York: A. S. Barnes. Reprint. Chicago: Rio Grande Press, 1964.

Barnes, Will C.
1941   *Apaches and Longhorns. The Reminiscences of Will C. Barnes.* Edited and with an introduction by Frank C. Lockwood. Los Angeles: Ward Ritchie Press.

Bartlett, Katharine and Colton, Harold S.
1940   "A Note on the Marcos de Niza Inscription near Phoenix, Arizona." *Plateau,* vol. 12, no. 4, April, pp. 53–59.

Benavente, Toribio Paredes de [Motolinía]
1941   *Historia de los Indios de la Nueva España.* Mexico City: Salvador Chávez Hayhoe.

Benavides, Alonso de
1945   "Fray Alonso de Benavides' Revised Memorial of 1634." With Numerous Supplementary Documents Elaborately Annotated by Frederick Webb Hodge, George P. Hammond, Agapito Rey. In *Coronado Cuarto Centennial Publications, 1540–1940*, vol. 4. Albuquerque: The University of New Mexico Press.
1962   "Memorial que Fray Juan de Santander de la Orden de San Francisco Comisario General de Indias, presenta a la Majestad del Rey Don Felipe Quarto Nuestro Señor. Hecho por el padre Fray Alonso de Benavides, 1630." In *Documentos para servir a la Historia del Nuevo México, 1538–1778*. Colección Chimalistac, no. 13. Madrid: Porrúa-Turanzas.

Bloom, Lansing B.
1940   "Who Discovered New Mexico?" *New Mexico Historical Review*, vol. 15, April, pp. 101–132.
1941   "Was Fray Marcos a Liar?" *New Mexico Historical Review*, vol. 16, April, pp. 244–246.

Bolton, Herbert Eugene
1971   *Coronado, Knight of Pueblos and Plains.* Albuquerque: University of New Mexico Press.

Burrus, Ernest J., S.J.
1969*a*   *A. F. Bandelier - A History of the Southwest: A Study of the Civilization and Conversion of the Indians in Southwestern United States and Northwestern Mexico from the Earliest Times to 1700. Vol. I. A Catalogue of the Bandelier Collection in the Vatican Library.* Sources and Studies for the History of the Americas: Vol. VII. Rome, St. Louis: Jesuit Historical Institute.
1969*b*   *A. F. Bandelier - A History of the Southwest: A Study of the Civilization and Conversion of the Indians in Southwestern United States and Northwestern Mexico from the Earliest Times to 1700. Supplement to Vol. I.* Sources and Studies for the History of the Americas: Vol. 8. Reproduction in Color of Thirty Sketches and of Ten Maps. Rome, St. Louis: Jesuit Historical Institute.

Bustamante, Pedro de
1864–1884   "Testimonio dado en México sobre el descubrimiento de doscientos Leguas adelante." In *Colección de documentos* ... , edited by J. Pacheco, F. de Cárdenas, *et al.*, vol. 15, pp. 80-88. Madrid. English translation by George P. Hammond and Agapito Rey, in *The Rediscovery of New Mexico, 1580–1594.* Coronado Cuarto Centennial Publications, 1540–1940. Vol. 3. Albuquerque: University of New Mexico Press, 1966.

Cabeza de Vaca
        See Núñez Cabeza de Vaca, Alvar.

Castañeda de Naçera, Pedro de
1896   "Relación de la Jornada de Cíbola." In *The Coronado Expedition, 1540–1542* by George Parker Winship, in *Fourteenth Annual Re-*

port of the Bureau of American Ethnology, 1892–1893. Part I. Washington: Government Printing Office. English translation by G. P. Winship in same volume.

Cervantes de Salazar, Francisco
1953   *Life in the Imperial and Loyal City of Mexico in New Spain and the Royal and Pontifical University of Mexico as described in the Dialogues for the Study of the Latin Language.* Prepared by Francisco Cervantes de Salazar for use in his classes and printed in 1554 by Juan Pablos. Published in facsimile with a translation by Minnie Lee Barrett Shepard, and an introduction and notes by Carlos Eduardo Castañeda. Austin: University of Texas Press. See also García-Icazbalceta 1939 for Spanish version.

Chávez, Angelico, O. F. M.
1968   *Coronado's Friars.* Washington, D.C.: Academy of American Franciscan History.

Coronado, Francisco Vásquez de
1864–1884   "Carta de Francisco Vázquez de Coronado al emperador, Dándole cuenta de la espedición a la provincia de Quivira, y de la inexactitud de lo referido a Fr. Marcos de Niza, acerca de aquel país, desta provincia de Tiguex, 20 octubre, 1541." In *Colección de documentos* . . . , edited by J. Pacheco, F. de Cárdenas, *et al.*, vol 3, pp. 363–369. Madrid. English translation by George P. Hammond and Agapito Rey, in *Narratives of the Coronado Expedition, 1540-1542.* Coronado Cuarto Centennial Publications, 1540–1940. Albuquerque: University of New Mexico Press, 1940. French translation by Henri Ternaux-Compans, in *Voyages, relations et mémoires.* . . . Vol. 9. Paris: A. Bertrand, 1837–41.

Coues, Elliott
1900   *On the Trail of a Spanish Pioneer: The Diary and Itinerary of Francisco Garcés.* 2 vols. New York: F. Harper.

Cuevas, Mariano, ed.
1975   *Documentos inéditos del siglo XVI para la historia de México.* Mexico City: Porrúa.

Cushing, Frank Hamilton
1893   "Outline of Zuñi Creation Myths." Introductory, *Thirteenth Annual Report of the Bureau of American Ethnology, 1891–1892.* Washington, D.C.: Government Printing Office.
1974   *Zuñi Fetiches.* Introduction by Tom Bahti. Facsimile Edition. Las Vegas, Nevada: K. C. Publications.
1979   See Green, Jesse.

Davis, W. W. H.
1869   *The Spanish Conquest of New Mexico.* Doylestown, Pennsylvania: Williams Watts Hart Davis.

114   *Madeleine Turrell Rodack*

Di Peso, Charles; Rinaldo, John B.; and Fenner, Gloria J.
1974   *Casas Grandes: A Fallen Trading Center of the Gran Chichimeca*, vol. 4. Dragoon: The Amerind Foundation; Flagstaff: Northland Press. 8 vols.

Fontana, Bernard L.
1960   "A Dedication to the Memory of Adolph F. A. Bandelier, 1840–1914." *Arizona and the West*, vol. 2, no. 1, Spring, pp. 1–5.

Garcés, Francisco, O. F. M.
1968   *Diario de exploraciones en Arizona y California en los años de 1775 y 1776: Introducción y notas de John Galvin*. Mexico City: UNAM. English translation by Elliot Coues. *On the Trail of a Spanish Pioneer: The Diary and Itinerary of Francisco Garcés*. New York: F. Harper, 1900.

García, Gregorio
1729   *Origen de los Indios de el Nuevo Mundo, e Indias Occidentales averiguado con discurso de opiniones por el padre presentado fr. Gregorio García, de la Orden de Predicadores*. 2d ed. Madrid: F. Martínez Abad.

García-Icazbalceta, Joaquín, ed.
1858, 1866   *Colección de documentos para la historia de México*. 2 vols. Mexico City: Antigua Librería.
1886–1892   *Nueva Colección de documentos para la historia de México*. 5 vols. Mexico City: Andrade y Morales.
1939   *México en 1554. Tres diálogos latinos por Francisco Cervantes de Salazar*. Translated by Joaquín García–Icazbalceta. Preliminary notes by Julio Jiménez Rueda. Biblioteca del Estudiante Universitario, no. 3. Mexico City: UNAM. English translation by Francisco Cervantes de Salazar in *Life in the Imperial and Loyal City of Mexico.* ... Austin: University of Texas Press, 1953.

Goad, Edgar F.
1939   "A Study of the Life of Adolph Francis Alphonse Bandelier, with an Appraisal of his Contributions to American Anthropology and Related Sciences." Ph.D. dissertation (unpublished). University of Southern California, Los Angeles.

Green, Jesse
1979   *Zuñi: Selected Writings of Frank Hamilton Cushing*. Lincoln: University of Nebraska Press.

Gusinde, Martin
1942–1943   "Fray Marcos de Niza Entdeckt New Mexico im Jahre 1539." *Ibero-Amerikanisches Archiv, XVI*, nos. 1, 2/3, 4, pp. 42–124.

Hakluyt, Richard
1904   *The Principall Navigations, Voyages, Traffiques and Discoveries of the English Nation, Made by Sea or Over-land to the Remote and Farthest*

Distant Quarters of the Earth at any Time within the Compasse of these 1600 Yeeres. [1589]. Vol. 9. Glasgow: James MacLehose and Sons. 12 vols.

Hallenback, Cleve
1949   *The Journey of Fray Marcos de Niza.* Dallas, Texas.

Hammond, George P.
1940   *Coronado's Seven Cities.* U.S. Coronado Exposition Commission. Albuquerque, New Mexico.

Hammond, George P. and Rey, Agapito, eds.
1940   *Narratives of the Coronado Expedition, 1540–1542.* Coronado Cuarto Centennial Publications, 1540–1940. Vol. 2. Albuquerque: University of New Mexico Press.
1966   *The Rediscovery of New Mexico, 1580–1594.* Coronado Cuarto Centennial Publications, 1540–1940. Vol. 3. Albuquerque: University of New Mexico Press.

Hartmann, William K. and Hartmann, Gayle H.
1972   "Juan de la Asunción, 1538: First Spanish Explorer of Arizona?" *The Kiva.* Arizona Archaeological and Historical Society, vol. 37, no. 2, Winter, pp. 93–103.

Haynes, Henry W.
1886   "Early Explorations of New Mexico." In *Narrative and Critical History of America,* edited by Justin Winsor, vol. 2, part 2, chapter 7, pp. 473–504. Boston: Houghton Mifflin.

Hedrick, Basil C.; Kelley, J. Charles; and Riley, Carroll L., eds.
1974   *The Mesoamerican Southwest: Readings in Archaeology, Ethnohistory and Ethnology.* Carbondale, Illinois: Southern Illinois University Press.

Herrera, Antonio de
1934–1957 *Historia General de los hechos de los Castellanos en las islas y tierra firme de el Mar Océano.* Con notas del Académico de número, Miguel Gómez del Campillo. Vols. 8, 12, 13, 14. Madrid. 17 vols.

Hewitt, Edgar L. and Bandelier, Adolph F.
1937   *Indians of the Río Grande Valley.* I. "The Río Grande Pueblos Today," by Edgar L. Hewett. II. "Documentary History of the Río Grande Pueblos," by Adolph F. Bandelier. Handbooks of Archaeological History. Albuquerque: University of New Mexico Press; Santa Fe: School of American Research.

Hobbs, Hulda R.
1940   "Bandelier in the Southwest." *El Palacio,* vol. 47, no. 6, June, pp. 121–136.

Hodge, Frederick W.
1895   "The First Discovered City of Cíbola." *American Anthropologist,* vol. 8, April, pp. 142–152.

1914   "Adolph Francis Alphonse Bandelier." *American Anthropologist*, vol. 16, no. 2, April-June, pp. 349–358.
1926   "The Six Cities of Cibola, 1581–1680." *New Mexico Historical Review*, vol. 1, October, pp. 478–488.
1932   "Biographical Sketch and Bibliography of Adolphe Francis Alphonse Bandelier." *New Mexico Historical Review*, vol. 7, no. 4, pp. 353–370.
1937   *History of Hawikuh, New Mexico: One of the So-called Cities of Cibola.* Publications of the Frederick Webb Hodge Anniversary Publication Fund, vol. 1. Los Angeles: The Southwest Museum.

Hodge, Frederick W. and Lewis, Theodore H.
1907   *Spanish Explorers in the Southwestern United States, 1528–1543.* New York: Scribner.

Holland, F. Ross
1969   *Hawikuh and the Seven Cities of Cibola.* Historical Background Study. Division of History, Office of Archaeology and Historic Preservation, National Park Service. Photo reproduced by National Technical Information Service, Washington, D.C.

Jaramillo, Juan
1896   "Account given by Captain Juan Jaramillo of the journey which he made to the New Country, on which Francisco Vázquez Coronado was the general." In *The Coronado Expedition, 1540–1542* by George Parker Winship, in *Fourteenth Annual Report of the Bureau of Ethnology, 1892–93. Part I.* Washington, D.C.: Government Printing Office. English translation by G. P. Winship in same volume.

Lange, Charles H.
1963   "Adolph F. Bandelier as a Pueblo Ethnologist." *The Kiva.* Arizona Archaeological and Historical Society, vol. 29, no. 1, October, pp. 28–34.

Lange, Charles H. and Riley, Carroll L., eds.
1966   *The Southwestern Journals of Adolph F. Bandelier, 1880–1882.* Albuquerque: University of New Mexico Press; Santa Fe: School of American Research.
1970   *The Southwestern Journals of Adolph F. Bandelier, 1883–1884.* Albuquerque: University of New Mexico Press.

Lange, Charles H.; Riley, Carroll L.; and Lange, Elizabeth M., eds.
1975   *The Southwestern Journals of Adolph F. Bandelier, 1885–1888.* Albuquerque: University of New Mexico Press; Santa Fe: School of American Research.

Las Casas, Bartolomé de
1974   *Brevíssima Relación de la destrucción de las Indias.* Preliminary note by Lic. F. G. de Cosío. Colección Metropolitana, no. 36. Mexico City: Departamento del Distrito Federal, Secretaria de Obras y Servicios. English translation: *The Devastation of the Indies*, by Herma Briffault. New York: Seabury Press.

Lettres édifiantes et curieuses
1781   Lettres écrites des Missions étrangères. New Edition. Mémoires
             d'Amérique, vol. 8. Paris: J. G. Merigot le Jeune. 26 vols. [Col-
             lected by C. le Gobien *et al.* and first published in Paris 1702–76.
             Rearranged and edited by Y.M.M.T. de Querbeuf.]

López de Gómara, Francisco
1954   *Historia general de las Indias.* "Hispania vitrix," cuya segunda parte
             corresponde a la Conquista de Méjico. Modernización del texto
             antiguo por Pilar Guibelalde, con unas notas prologales de
             Emiliano M. Aguilera. 2 vols. Barcelona: Iberia.

Lowery, Woodbury
1901   *The Spanish Settlements within the Present Limits of the United States,*
             1513–1561. New York, London: Putnam.

Manje, Juan Mateo
1926   *Luz de Tierra Incógnita en la América Septentrional y diario de las*
             exploraciones en Sonora. Revision, notes and index by Francisco
             Fernández del Castillo. Mexico City: Publicaciones del Archivo
             General de la Nación. English translation of Part II: *Unknown*
             Arizona and Sonora 1693–1721, by Harry J. Karns and associates.
             Tucson: Arizona Silhouettes, 1954.

Mendieta, Gerónimo de
1971   *Historia Ecclesiastica Indiana,* 4 vols. Mexico City: Porrúa.

Mendoza, Antonio de
1864–1884   "Carta al emperador, 17 abril, 1540." In *Colección de documentos*
             . . . , edited by J. Pacheco, F. de Cárdenas, *et al.*, vol. 15, pp. 80–88.
             Madrid. French translation by Henri Ternaux-Compans, in *Voy-*
             ages, relations et mémoires. . . . Vol. 9. Paris: A. Bertrand, 1837–41.
             English translation by George P. Hammond, and Agapito Rey, in
             Narratives of the Coronado Expedition, 1540–1542. Albuquerque:
             University of New Mexico Press, 1940.

Morgan, Lewis H.
1869   "The Seven Cities of Cíbola." *North American Review,* vol. 18,
             April, pp. 456–498.
1881   *Houses and House-life of the American Aborigines.* Contributions to
             North American Ethnology, vol. 4. Washington, D.C.: Govern-
             ment Printing Office.

Mota-Padilla, Matías Angel de la
1973   *Historia de la conquista del reino de la Nueva Galicia en la América*
             Septentrional. Adicionada y comentada por José Ireneo Gutiérrez.
             Instituto Nacional de Antropología e Historia. Guadalajara: Uni-
             versidad de Guadalajara.

Navarrete, Martín Fernández de
1945   *Colección de los Viages y Descubrimientos que hicieron por Mar los Es-*
             pañoles desde fines del Siglo XV. Vol. 3. Buenos Aires: Guaranía.
             5 vols.

Nentwig, Juan, S. J.
1971   *Descripción geográfica, natural y curiosa de la Provincia de Sonora por un amigo de el Servicio de Dios de el Rey Nuestro Señor [Rudo Ensayo]*, edited by Germán Viveros. Mexico: Publicaciones Archivo General de la Nación. Series 2, no. 1.

Niza, Marcos de, O. F. M.
1864–1884   "Descubrimiento de las siete ciudades por el P. Fr. Marcos de Niza." ["Relación"] 1. Instrucción de Don Antonio de Mendoza. 2. Certificaciones. 3. Relación. 4. Legalización. In *Colección de documentos ...*, edited by J. Pacheco, F. de Cárdenas, *et al.*, vol. 3. Madrid. English translation by George P. Hammond, and Agapito Rey, in *Narratives of the Coronado Expedition, 1540–1542*. Albuquerque: University of New Mexico Press, 1940. See also Oblasser 1939 and Baldwin 1926.

Norton, E. W. T., ed.
1912   *Centennial History of Madison County, Illinois and its People, 1812–1912*. 2 vols. Chicago and New York: The Lewis Publishing Co.

Núñez Cabeza de Vaca, Alvar
1946   *Naufragios y Comentarios*. 2d ed. Colección Austral. Buenos Aires and Mexico City: Espasa-Calpe. English translation by Buckingham Smith, ed., *Naufragios: Relation of Alvar Nuñez Cabeza de Vaca*. New York, 1871. See also Bandelier, Fanny Ritter 1905.

Oblasser, Bonaventure, O. F. M.
1939   *His Own Personal Narrative of Arizona Discovered by Fray Marcos de Niza who in 1539 First Entered These Parts on his Quest for the Seven Cities of Cibola*. Topowa, Arizona.

Obregón, Balthasar de
1924   *Historia de los descubrimientos antiguos y modernos de la Nueva España*. Written in 1584. Edited by Mariano Cuevas. Mexico City: Departamento Editorial de la Secretaria de Educación. English translation: *Obregón's History of Sixteenth Century Exploration in Western America* by George Hammond and Agapito Rey, eds. Los Angeles: Wetzel Publishing Co., 1928.

Orozco y Berra, Manuel
1864   *Geografía de las lenguas y una carta etnográfica de México*. Mexico City: Imp. de Andrade y Escalante.

Oviedo y Valdés, Gonzalo Fernández de
1945   *Historia general y natural de las Indias, islas y tierra-firme del mar océano*. Prólogo de J. Natalicio González, Notas de José Amador de los Ríos. Vols. 5, 10. Asunción del Paraguay: Guaranía. 14 vols.

Pacheco, Joaquín; Cárdenas, Francisco de; *et al.*, eds.
1864–1884   *Colección de documentos inéditos relativos al descubrimiento, conquista y organización de las posesiones españoles en América y Oceania, sacados, en su mayor parte del Real Archivo de Indias*. Vols. 2, 3, 15, 16. Madrid. 42 vols.

Pérez de Ribas, Andrés, S.J.
1944   *Historia de los Triumfos de Nuestra Santa Fe entre gentes las más bár-
            baras y fieras del Nuevo Orbe.* 2 vols. México: Layac. Partial English
            translation in condensed form: *My Life Among the Savage Nations
            of New Spain,* by Tomás Antonio Robertson. Los Angeles: Ward
            Ritchie Press, 1968.

Pimentel, Francisco
1862–1865   *Cuadro descriptivo y comparativo de las lenguas indígenas de México.*
            2 vols. Mexico City: Imp. de Andrade y Escalante.

Ramusio, Giovanni Battista
1563–1565   *Navigatione et viaggi raccolto gia da m. Gio. Battista Ramusio.* Vol.
            3. Venezia: Giunti. 3 vols.

Riley, Carroll L.
1963   "Adolph F. Bandelier as Archaeologist." *The Kiva,* vol. 29, no. 1,
            October, pp. 23–27.
1971   "Early Spanish-Indian Communication in the Greater South-
            west." *New Mexico Historical Review,* vol. 46, no. 4, October, pp.
            289–293.
1972   "Blacks in the Early Southwest." *Ethnohistory,* vol. 9, no. 3 Sum-
            mer, pp. 247–260.
1975   "The Road to Hawikuh: Trade and Trade Routes to Cíbola-Zuñi
            during Late Prehistoric and Early Historic Times." *The Kiva,* vol.
            41, no. 2, Winter, pp. 137–159.

Rodack, Madeleine
1979   "The 'Lost' Manuscript of Adolph Bandelier." *New Mexico Histor-
            ical Review,* vol. 54, no. 3, July, pp. 183–207.

Rudo Ensayo
            See Nentwig 1971.

Sauer, Carl O.
1932   *The Road to Cibola.* Berkeley: University of California Press.
1937   "The Discovery of New Mexico Reconsidered." *New Mexico His-
            torical Review,* vol. 12, July, pp. 270–287.
1941   "The Credibility of the Fray Marcos Account." *New Mexico His-
            torical Review,* vol. 16, April, pp. 233–246.

Schroeder, Albert E.
1955   "Fray Marcos de Niza, Coronado and the Yavapai." *New Mexico
            Historical Review,* vol. 30, no. 4, October, pp. 265–296; *ibid.* vol.
            31, no. 1, January, pp. 24–37.

Shaefer, Jack Warner
1966   *Adolphe Francis Alphonse Bandelier.* Series of Western Americana,
            no. 7. Santa Fe: The Press of the Territorian.

Simpson, James Harvey
1871   "Coronado's March in Search of the 'Seven Cities of Cibola' and
            Discussion of their Probable Location." *Report of the Smithsonian*

120   *Madeleine Turrell Rodack*

Institution for 1869, pp. 309–340. Washington, D.C.: Government Printing Office.

Spencer, A. P., ed.
1937   *Centennial History of Highland, Illinois, 1837–1937.* Highland, Illinois: Centennial Commission. Reprint. Highland, Ill.: Highland Historical Society, 1978.

Spier, Leslie
1917   "An Outline for a Chronology of Zuñi Ruins." *Anthropological Papers of the American Museum of Natural History.* Vol. 18, part 3. New York.

Stocklein, Joseph, ed.
1726   "Allerhand so Lehr als Geist reiche Brief, Schrifften und Reis-Beschreibungen, welche von denen Missionariis der Gesellschaft Jesu aus Beyden Indien und anderen über Meer gelegenen Ländern." Seit Án. 1642 bis auf das Jahr 1726 in Europa angelangt seynd jetzt zum erstenmal. Verteutscht und zusammen getragen von Joseph Stocklein, gedachter Societat Jesu Priester. In *Der Neue Weltbott,* vol. I–8. Augsburg und Gratz: in Verlag Phillips, Martins und Joh. Veith seel. Erben, Buchhändlern.

Stoner, Victor R., S.J.
1939   "The Discovery of Arizona." *The Kiva,* vol. 4, no. 1, April 1939, pp. 27–30.

Swiss-American Historical Society
1932   *Prominent Americans of Swiss Origin: A Compilation prepared by the Swiss-American Historical Society.* New York: James T. White and Co.

Tello, Antonio
1858,1866   *Fragmentos de una Historia de la Nueva Galicia, escrita hácia 1650 por el Padre Fray Antonio Tello de la Orden de San Francisco.* Colección de documentos Mexico City: Antigua Librería. . . . , edited by Joaquín García-Icazbalceta, vol. 2, pp. 343–458.

Ternaux-Compans, Henri
1837–1841   *Voyages, relations et mémoires originaux pour servir à l'histoire de la découverte de l'Amérique, publiés pour la première fois en français.* Vols. 9, 18, 19. Paris: A. Bertrand. 20 vols.

Terrell, John Upton
1968   *Estevanico the Black.* Los Angeles: Westernlore Press.

Tibesar, Antonio, O. F. M.
1953   *Franciscan Beginnings in Colonial Peru.* Washington, D.C.: Academy of American-Franciscan History.

Torquemada, Juan de
1975   *Monarchia Indiana.* Introducción por Miguel León Portilla. 3 vols. México: Porrúa.

Twitchell, Ralph Emerson
1911–1917   *The Leading Facts of New Mexican History.* Vol. 1. Cedar Rapids, Iowa: The Torch Press. 5 vols.

Undreiner, George J.
1947   "Fray Marcos de Niza and his Journey to Cíbola." *The Americas,* vol. 3, April, pp. 415–486.

Velasco, Juan de
1961   *Historia del Reyno de Quito en la América Meridional.* Texto establecido por Aurelio Espinosa Pólit. 2 vols. Puebla: J. M. Cajica, Jr. French translation by Henri Ternaux-Compans, *Voyages, relations et mémoires....* Vols, 18, 19. Paris: A. Bertrand, 1837–41.

Vetancurt, Agustín de
1961   "Menologio Franciscano de los varones más señalados que con sus vidas exemplares ilustraron la Provincia de el Santo Evangelio de México." In *Teatro Mexicano.* Vol. 4. Colección Chimalistac, no. 11. Madrid: Porrúa–Turanzas. 4 Vols.

Wagner, Henry R.
1934   "Fray Marcos de Niza." *New Mexico Historical Review,* vol. 9, April, pp. 184–227.
1937   *The Spanish Southwest, 1542–1794.* The Quivira Society, vol. 7, parts 1, 2. Albuquerque: University of New Mexico Press. Reprint. New York: Arno Press, 1967.

White, Leslie A., ed.
1940   *Pioneers in American Anthropology: The Bandelier-Morgan Letters, 1873–1883.* 2 vols. Albuquerque: University of New Mexico Press.

White, Leslie A. and Bernal, Ignacio, eds.
1960   *Correspondencia de Adolfo F. Bandelier. I. La Interpretación Morgan–Bandelier de la Sociedad Azteca. II. Correspondencia Bandelier-García-Icazbalceta.* Instituto Nacional de Antropología e Historia, Serie Historia, VI. Mexico City: INAH.

Winship, George P.
1895   "Why Coronado went to New Mexico in 1540." In *Annual Report of the American Historical Association for 1894,* pp. 83–92. Washington, D.C.: Government Printing Office.
1896   "The Coronado Expedition, 1540–1542." In *Fourteenth Annual Report of the Bureau of American Ethnology, 1892–1893. Part I.* Washington, D.C.: Government Printing Office.

Winsor, Justin (ed.)
1886   *Narrative and Critical History of America.* Vol. 2, part 1, 2; vol. 3, part 1. Boston: Houghton Mifflin. 8 vols.

Ximénez de San Esteban, Jerónimo
1886–1892   "Carta a Santo Tomás de Villanueva, 9 octubre 1539." In *Nueva Colección de documentos para la historia de México,* edited by J.

García-Icazbalceta, vol. 1. Mexico City: Andrade y Morales. English translation by Henry R. Wagner, in *The Spanish Southwest, 1542–1794*, part 1. Albuquerque: University of New Mexico Press, 1937.

Zárate-Salmerón, Gerónimo
1962   "Relaciones de todas las cosas que en el Nuevo-México se han visto y savido, asi por mar como por tierra, desde el año de 1538 hasta el de 1626." In *Documentos para servir a la Historia de Nuevo México, 1528–1778*. Colección Chimalistac, no. 13. Madrid: Porrúa-Turanzas.

Zumárraga, Juan de
1886–1892 "Tres cartas familiares de Fr. Juan de Zumárraga, primer obispo y arzobispo de México; y contestación a otra que le dirige Fr. Marcos de Niza." In *Nueva Colección de documentos para la historia de México*, edited by J. García-Icazbalceta, vol. 2. Mexico City: Andrade y Morales.
1975   "Carta al emperador." In *Documentos inéditos del siglo XVI para la historia de México*, edited by Mariano Cuevas, pp. 83–84. Mexico City: Porrúa.

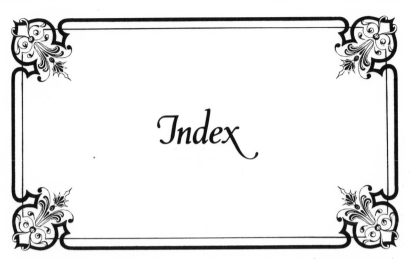

Index

[123]

Doguenes (Indians), 57 n. 8
Dorantes, Andrés, 31, 44, 56 n. 6

Edwardsville, Illinois, 21
El Carrizo (Salt lake in New Mexico), 97
El Morro National Monument, New Mexico, 36
Emeralds: given Cabeza de Vaca by Indians, 54
Encomienda system, 67
Española, 56 n. 6. *See also* Hispaniola
Espejo, Antonio de, 61 n. 35, 92, 102 n. 2, 103 n. 23; *Relación del Viaje*, quoted, 61 n. 33
Espíritu-Santo, Bay of, 60 n. 26
Espíritu-Santo, Río del, 60 n. 26. *See also* Mississippi River
Estevan: arrival in Cíbola, 86–87; assigned to Fray Marcos expedition, 33, 69–70; available for expedition to North, 31; death of, 87, 95; Castañeda comments on, 76; Fray Marcos' instructions to, 74; importance of, 39, 98; leaves shelters and messages for Fray Marcos, 86; sends messages to Fray Marcos, 75, 76; survivor of Narváez expedition, 44
Estevanico. *See* Estevan
Estrada, Alonso de, 66
Estufas (kivas), 99
Eudeve (language), 62 n. 39, 74
Eudeves (Indians), 61–62 n. 39, 53

F. Ryhiner & Co., 18, 20–21
Fish: eaten by Indians, 56 n. 7, 57, n. 9
Florida, 46, 50, 57 n. 12
Food, Native. *See* Beans; Corn; Fish; Indians, food and supplies; Marrow; Mezquite; Squash
Fort Apache, Arizona: Bandelier

arrives at, 23, 45 n; distance to Zuñi and Río Gila, 103 n. 16
Fort Craig, New Mexico, 52, 61 n. 35
Fort Grant, Arizona, 80
Fray Marcos Inscription. *See* Niza, Fray Marcos de: inscription
Fronteras, Sonora, 83 n. 36

Garcés, Fray Francisco, 32
Gila, Río: distances from Fort Apache and San Pedro River, 103 n. 16; Pima villages along, 54. *See also* Gila River
Gila River: distance from Zuñi, 90; possible discovery of, 33, 69; possibly on Fray Marcos' route, 80, 85. *See also* Gila, Río
Gold: identified by Indians, 73; Indians said to have, 72; Fray Marcos told of, 38; Spanish search for, 27
Gregorian Calendar, 58 n. 20, 70 n, 72 n
Gregory XIII (pope), 70 n
Gruaz, Timothy, 18
Guacamayos. See Macaws
Guatemala, 29, 67 n
Guaycones (Indians), 57 n. 8
Guaymas (Indians), 82 n. 23
Guaymas, Puerto de, 77
Guevenes (Indians), 57 n. 8
Gusinde, Martin, 34
Guzmán, Nuño de, 58 n. 20, 65, 66, 68; *Primera Relación Anónima de la Jornada de Nuño de Guzmán*, quoted, 81 n. 2; *Segunda Relación de la Jornada de Nuño de Guzmán*, quoted, 81 n. 2

Ha-cu, 96. *See also* Aco; Acoma; Acus
Ha-cu-quin, 96. *See also* Aco; Acoma, Acus
Haemish (Jemez), 94
Hallenback, Cleve, 38

Tello, Fray Antonio: *Historia de la Nueva Galicia,* quoted, 58 n. 19
Tenochtitlan: gold found in, 27; Qaquima compared to, 100; size of, 104 n. 46
Te-tzo-ge. *See* Tezuque
Texas, 46, 50, 52, 60 n. 29
Tezuque, 103 n. 30
Thomson, Robert. *See* Tomson
Thunder Mesa, 92. *See also* Thunder Mountain; Toyoalana; Zuñi Mesa
Thunder Mountain, 34, 91. *See also* Thunder Mesa; Toyoalana, Zuñi Mesa
Tibesar, Antonine: *Franciscan Beginnings in Colonial Peru,* cited, 30
Tiburón Island, 76
Tlatelolco, 100–101
Tomson, Robert (Thomson), 104 n. 47
Tonteac, 82 n. 27. *See also* Totonteac
Topax (Iopax), 89 n
Torquemada, Fray Juan de: *Monarchía Indiana,* 32
Torres, Diego de, 66
Totonteac, 104 n. 37; gray cloth worn at, 79, 99; identified with Moqui, 97, 100; "kingdom" near Cíbola, 76. *See also* Tonteac
To-ya. *See* Nutria
Toyoalana, 34, 35, 91, 103 n. 32. *See also* Thunder Mesa; Thunder Mountain; Zuñi Mesa
Trade. *See* Indians: trade
Trinity River (Texas), 60 n. 29
Tucson, Arizona, 35, 36, 80, 94
Tuna (cactus fruit), 46, 50, 52, 57 n. 9
Turquoises: given to Cabeza de Vaca's party, 54; possessed by natives, 47, 53; received by Indians for work in Cíbola, 76;

used to ornament houses, 75, 99; worn by natives, 78, 99
Tusayan, 102 n. 2

Undreiner, George J.: "Fray Marcos de Niza and his Journey to Cibola," 36
Ures, 47 n

Vaca de Castro, 68 n
Vacapa: Fray Marcos arrives at, 73–74; Fray Marcos leaves, 76; location of, 35, 73–74; origin of name, 73
Vacas, Río de las, 51. *See also* "Cow River"; Pecos, Río
Valencia, Fray Martín de (Martín de Buil), 66 n
Valladolid, Spain, 45, 56 n. 6
Vargas, Diego de, 36, 103 n. 19
Venezuela, 21
Vera-Paz, Bishop of. *See* Angulo, Pedro de
Vetancurt, Fray Agustín de: *Crónica [de la Provincia del Santo Evangelio],* quoted, 104 n. 41; *Menologio Franciscano,* on Fray Marcos, 29, 55 n. 1; *Menologio,* on early explorations in North, 32
Villanueva, Father Tomás, 28
Villard Expedition, 22
Visita: definition of, 104 n. 41

Wagner, Henry: *The Spanish Southwest,* 29
Walker, John D. (judge), 62 n. 41
Wichita Mountains (Indian Territory), 60 n. 31

Ximénez de San Esteban, Fray, 28

Yaqui (language), 72